.NET 7 for Jobseekers

Elevate your coding journey with .NET 7

Filipe Vilhena

bpb

www.bpbonline.com

Copyright © 2023 BPB Online

All rights reserved. No part of this book may be reproduced, stored in a retrieval system, or transmitted in any form or by any means, without the prior written permission of the publisher, except in the case of brief quotations embedded in critical articles or reviews.

Every effort has been made in the preparation of this book to ensure the accuracy of the information presented. However, the information contained in this book is sold without warranty, either express or implied. Neither the author, nor BPB Online or its dealers and distributors, will be held liable for any damages caused or alleged to have been caused directly or indirectly by this book.

BPB Online has endeavored to provide trademark information about all of the companies and products mentioned in this book by the appropriate use of capitals. However, BPB Online cannot guarantee the accuracy of this information.

First published: 2023

Published by BPB Online
WeWork
119 Marylebone Road
London NW1 5PU

UK | UAE | INDIA | SINGAPORE

ISBN 978-93-55518-224

www.bpbonline.com

Dedicated to

My beloved wife:
Sónia

&

*My Son **Afonso***

About the Author

Filipe Vilhena is a software developer with nearly 17 years of experience, having worked in different companies and projects, in the banking and insurance area, in Portugal, and delivering projects using different Microsoft Technologies, such as ASP.net, C#, VB.net, T-SQL, Integration Services, Reporting Services, javascript, JQuery and others.

At the moment, he is working as a DevOps Engineer in Axa Partners Portugal, developing several in-house application for insurance, assistance and internal management. He is also working with Agile methodologies and helping to spread them throughout the company.

He finished his degree of studies in Escola Superior de Tecnologia de Setúbal, in 2007, and has since taken a few courses in Microsoft.

In his spare time, he loves to travel and spend quality time with his family (and his kitten!), whenever possible. Also, he's a fan of cinema, music, photography, and an eager reader, who loves a good thriller, being also a huge Nordic Noir fan!

About the Reviewer

Abhishek Jain is a passionate programmer with extensive professional experience in developing Large-Scale application with Microsoft technologies, Angular and other native language, Application fitment for cloud, Cloud Operating Model, Cloud Vendor Evaluation, Cloud Policy and Cloud Economics. He is an holder of multiple industry operation knowledge which enhance experience in understand workflow and in understand level of work to be done.

Abhishek specializes in Data Science and FinOps and loves working with customers on helping them in getting the most out of their cloud investment.

He is currently working as Senior Solution Architect in USA Company.

Acknowledgement

I would like to thank in the first place, to my family, Sónia and Afonso, for their strong support and encouragement and also for their patience when I was writing until late hours after work, and investigating for this book.

I would also like to thank my parents António and Otilia, and all my family for turning me into the people I am and for helping me to learn and study and evolve as a person.

I am also grateful to BPB Publications, it was a long journey of investigation, writing, and revising this book, with valuable participation and collaboration of reviewers, technical experts, and editors.

I am also thankful to my teachers at Escola Secundária da Moita and Escola Superior de Tecnologia de Setúbal, who helped me and inspired me to follow this career, namely: my teacher Anabela from 12th-grade Physics and my Faculty teachers Adelaide Trabuco, Nuno Pina, Alpesh Ranchordas, Rui Madeira and Hugo Gamboa.

I would also like to thank the contributions of my colleagues and co-worker during many years working in the tech industry, who have taught me so much and guided me into learning what I know now and helped me to gain experience to write this book. Also, a special thanks to my colleague Edgar Elias, that also served as a reviewer for this book, and who gave me some insights on the matter.

Finally, I would like to thank all the readers who have interest in this book and in learning more.

Preface

Working with .net technologies is quite an interesting task and, since it is always evolving, it is a great challenge to learn more and more everyday.

This book is designed to provide a guide to what .Net is, how it is evolving and what is new in this .Net 7 version. It covers a wide range of topics, including knowledge about MVC, Razor, Blazor, .Net MAUI, Orleans and more.

Throughout the book, you will learn the basics and a bit of history on .Net framework, and will get to know more about different functionalities and improvements that .Net 7 brings.

This book is intended for the ones who want to learn about .Net and mainly its latest version of .Net 7, so it will help them in their always challenging task of Job seeking.

With this book, you will gain the knowledge and skills to learn how .Net 7 works and what it brings as new. I hope you will find this book informative and helpful.

Chapter 1: Introduction to .Net 7- will make a quick introduction to the environment and framework, in order to understand a bit of the story behind it and how did it get to this version 7. It will contain examples of the existing framework and what it covers now.

Chapter 2: New Features and Libraries - will review this framework version and all the new features and libraries implemented, regarding the last stable framework (.net 6). It will be illustrated with a few samples of the features.

Chapter 3: Writing Your First .Net 7 Program – covers, in a small walkthrough, all the steps to create a simple program with the Hello World typical example, using this new .net 7 framework. It will be created in a simple way using Razor pages.

Chapter 4: Designing the Views - will explain in a simple way how to create some views of a .net 7 application.

Chapter 5: Creating Your Controllers - will explain in a simple way how to create the controllers for a .net 7 application, giving some examples of an application. It will show how the controller can connect with the Views.

Chapter 6: Testing Your Views and Controllers- will go through the way to test the connection and use of the Views and controllers.

Chapter 7: Working with .Net MAUI - explains what is .Net MAUI and how to use this new App UI. It will show some examples of possible integrations. It will also explain what are the Operating Systems and platforms on which it will be implemented.

Chapter 8: Blazor in .Net7 - is dedicated to learn what is Blazor and the improvements it has in .Net 7. It will show some examples and some different ways to use it.

Chapter 9: Creating a Desktop UI – after learning about MAUI it is dedicated to learn how to create a desktop UI and to use a bit of WinForms.

Chapter 10: Communication with the Views - is dedicated to explain how to communicate between UI and the Views created in chapter 4.

Chapter 11: Use SignalR - explains what is SignalR, what's the improvements on .Net 7 and how to use it.

Chapter 12: Adding a Database - explains how to add a database and how to connect it to this model using .net 7.

Chapter 13: Orleans - explains what is Orleans, how to use it and what it has new in .Net 7.

Chapter 14: Adding Specific Code Using System.Devices - will explain how to add specific code with System.Devices and this new framework.

Chapter 15: Possible Questions and Answers - will go through some possible questions when landing a .Net role and provide some answers.

Code Bundle and Coloured Images

Please follow the link to download the
Code Bundle and the *Coloured Images* of the book:

https://rebrand.ly/dpljvfh

The code bundle for the book is also hosted on GitHub at **https://github.com/bpbpublications/.NET-7-for-Jobseekers**. In case there's an update to the code, it will be updated on the existing GitHub repository.

We have code bundles from our rich catalogue of books and videos available at **https://github.com/bpbpublications**. Check them out!

Errata

We take immense pride in our work at BPB Publications and follow best practices to ensure the accuracy of our content to provide with an indulging reading experience to our subscribers. Our readers are our mirrors, and we use their inputs to reflect and improve upon human errors, if any, that may have occurred during the publishing processes involved. To let us maintain the quality and help us reach out to any readers who might be having difficulties due to any unforeseen errors, please write to us at :

errata@bpbonline.com

Your support, suggestions and feedbacks are highly appreciated by the BPB Publications' Family.

Did you know that BPB offers eBook versions of every book published, with PDF and ePub files available? You can upgrade to the eBook version at www.bpbonline.com and as a print book customer, you are entitled to a discount on the eBook copy. Get in touch with us at :

business@bpbonline.com for more details.

At **www.bpbonline.com**, you can also read a collection of free technical articles, sign up for a range of free newsletters, and receive exclusive discounts and offers on BPB books and eBooks.

Piracy

If you come across any illegal copies of our works in any form on the internet, we would be grateful if you would provide us with the location address or website name. Please contact us at **business@bpbonline.com** with a link to the material.

If you are interested in becoming an author

If there is a topic that you have expertise in, and you are interested in either writing or contributing to a book, please visit **www.bpbonline.com**. We have worked with thousands of developers and tech professionals, just like you, to help them share their insights with the global tech community. You can make a general application, apply for a specific hot topic that we are recruiting an author for, or submit your own idea.

Reviews

Please leave a review. Once you have read and used this book, why not leave a review on the site that you purchased it from? Potential readers can then see and use your unbiased opinion to make purchase decisions. We at BPB can understand what you think about our products, and our authors can see your feedback on their book. Thank you!

For more information about BPB, please visit **www.bpbonline.com**.

Join our book's Discord space

Join the book's Discord Workspace for Latest updates, Offers, Tech happenings around the world, New Release and Sessions with the Authors:

https://discord.bpbonline.com

Table of Contents

1. **Introduction to .Net 7** 1
   Introduction 1
   Structure 2
   A small piece of .Net history 2
   Examples of .Net 6 4
       Middleware integration 4
       Routing 5
       Add Services 6
   Conclusion 7

2. **New Features and Libraries** 9
   Introduction 9
   New features of this framework 10
       Blazor 10
       New loading page 11
       Data binding modifiers 11
       Virtualization improvements 12
       Navigation manager 12
       Additional cryptography support 13
       New problem details service 13
       Diagnostics middleware updates 13
       Minimal API 13
       Typed results 14
       OpenAPI improvements 15
       Self-describing minimal APIs 15
       Return multiple result types 16
       MVC 17
       Links 17

New libraries 18
    Nullable annotations for Microsoft.Extensions 18
    System.Text.RegularExpressions improvements
    and new APIs 19
    LibraryImportGenerator 19
.Net 6 vs .Net 7 20
    Blazor and .Net MAUI 20
    Cloud native and containers 21
    Json 22
    JWT authentication configuration 23
    C#11 24
Conclusion 26

3. Writing Your First .Net 7 Program 27
Introduction 27
Structure 27
Creating a .Net 7 project\solution 28
Adding and configuring pages 33
    Changing view Index.cshtml 34
    Navigate through the Solution Explorer 35
    Use minimal APIs 36
    Add pages and interact between pages 37
Implementing the project 41
Conclusion 43

4. Designing the Views 45
Introduction 45
Structure 45
Objectives 46
Creating the Views 46
    MVC 46
    Razor pages 50

      Creating a partial view 52
      MVC 53
      Razor pages 58
   Conclusion 61

5. Creating Your Controllers 63
   Introduction 63
   Structure 63
   Objectives 64
   Creating a simple Controller 64
   Integrating the Controller with the View 67
   Creating and using a Model 71
      Adding a Model Class 72
   Conclusion 76

6. Testing Your Views and Controllers 77
   Introduction 77
   Structure 77
   Objectives 78
   Unit tests 78
   Performing tests and debug 80
   Advantages of unit tests 81
   Conclusion 82

7. Working with .NET MAUI 83
   Introduction 83
   Structure 84
   Objectives 84
   .Net MAUI in a nutshell 85
   New functionalities in .Net MAUI 87
      Maps 87
      Desktop improvements 88

Using .Net MAUI in a .Net 7 application 91

Different libraries and platform specific frameworks 96

Conclusion 98

8. Blazor in .NET 7 99

Introduction 99

Structure 100

Objectives 100

An introduction to Blazor in .Net 7 100

New in Blazor for .Net 7 103

A Bit on Blazor Hybrid 105

Sharing code and libraries 106

JavaScript Interop 106

Conclusion 110

9. Creating a Desktop UI 113

Introduction 113

Structure 114

Objectives 114

Desktop UI 114

    WinUI on .Net MAUI 115

    Other desktop applications - Win32 116

    Other desktop applications – Windows Forms 117

Creating a WinUI 3 project 117

Windows forms improvements in .Net 7 123

Conclusion 126

10. Communication with the Views 127

Introduction 127

Structure 128

Objectives 128

Ways of communicating with the views 128

How a controller calls a view 129
　　　　　Pass data to views 131
　　Model-View-Controller 136
　　Model-View-ViewModel (MVVM) 138
　　Conclusion 139

11. Use SignalR 141
　　Introduction 141
　　Structure 142
　　Objectives 142
　　What is SignalR and how to use it 142
　　　How SignalR works in ASP.Net Core applications 143
　　　The HubConnection class 144
　　Advantages of SignalR 146
　　What can you do with ASP.Net and SignalR 147
　　Improvements in .Net 7 152
　　Conclusion 154

12. Adding a Database 155
　　Introduction 155
　　Structure 156
　　Objectives 156
　　　Adding the database 156
　　Ways of using databases 160
　　Entity framework 7 161
　　New interceptors and events in EF 163
　　JSON columns 164
　　Custom database first templates 166
　　Conclusion 166

13. Orleans 167
　　Introduction 167

Structure 168
Objectives 168
What is Orleans 168
How and where to use Orleans 169
What is new in Orleans in .Net 7 179
Conclusion 182

14. Adding Specific Code Using System.Devices 183
Introduction 183
Structure 183
Objectives 184
System.Devices 184
Conclusion 196

15. Possible Questions and Answers 197
Introduction 197
Structure 198
Objectives 198
Possible questions and answers 198
Conclusion 204

Index 205-209

CHAPTER 1
Introduction to .Net 7

Introduction

Programming today is something that can be done in more simpler ways. The days where it is a huge mess and lots of trouble to make a simple program are now gone.

Microsoft created the .Net programming environment and the .Net Framework, which already contains several class libraries and provides language interoperability between several programming languages (C#, VB.net, F# and others, like C++, J#, Jscript.Net, IronPython or IronRuby).

This framework, or abstraction, contains generic functionalities that are executed on a CLR, providing user interface, data access, database connectivity, cryptography, web application development, numeric algorithms, and network communications. All of this can be combined in the source code that is created by programmers and software engineers, also with other libraries that are available.

It allows developers to create cloud apps, console apps, web apps, APIs, desktop apps, games, mobile apps, windows apps, machine learning, and IoT applications.

.Net has a large set of class libraries which facilitate these developments and can be used in this different project types. For example, we can use `System.Object` from which every .Net type derives, primitive types like `System.Boolean`, some collections such as `System.Collections.Generic.List<T>`, file and stream IO (`System.IO.FileStream`), JSON or XML serialization (`System.Text.Json.JsonSerializer` and `System.IO.TextWriter`). Also, if you need other different packages, you can use NuGet Package Manager to download and add them to your project.

Structure

In this chapter we will discuss following topics:

- A small piece of history on .Net
- Show some examples of the current release (.Net 6)
- Share a bit of the evolution of this platform

A small piece of .Net history

.Net Framework began its journey in late 1990s, under the name of Next Generation Windows Services. The first beta version of .Net 1.0 was released in early 2000. C# and the CLI were standardized in August 2000.

Two years later (in 2002), was the celebration of the first official .Net Framework release (which turns 20 years this year).

Later, in October 2007, the source code for .Net Framework 3.5 libraries was launched and became available online in January next year, including, BCL, ASP.Net, ADO.Net, Windows Forms, WPF and XML. (*This was one of the first frameworks on which I've worked!*).

But things changed in 2014, with the introduction of .Net Core as a cross-platform and successor to .Net Framework. The name .Net Core was maintained until .Net Core 3.1 being replaced with only .Net upon the release of version 5, which followed 3.1 and skipped directly to 5 to avoid confusion with framework versions.

So, this .Net version is a core version and does not replace the framework, but includes several improvements and updates in C#, F# and Visual Basic, new JSON features, single file apps, annotation on 80% of nullable reference types and improvements in JSON, Garbage Collection, RegEx, Async and many more areas.

Afterwards, in November 2021, another .Net Version came out: release 6. This was the final part of the unification plan that started with the earlier version. .Net 6 unifies SDK, base libraries, and runtimes across mobile, desktop, IoT and cloud apps. It also includes simplified development, better performance, and ultimate productivity.

Yet another very important news in .Net 6 is the introduction of a C# source generator to improve performance of applications that use **System.Text.Json**. It will help and simplify Json Serialization – and can be seen in detail over at Microsoft DevBlogs **https://devblogs. microsoft.com/dotnet/try-the-new-system-text-json-source-generator/**.

Other improvements of version 6 include: date, time and time zone improvements, new LINQ

APIs, Microsoft Extensions API, Reflection APIs, Generic Math and much more (all these functionalities and information are available on Microsoft documentation site **https://docs.microsoft.com/en-us/ dotnet/core/whats-new/dotnet-6**).

One of the biggest improvements was a rewrite of **System. IO.FileStream** that now simplifies asynchronous I/O on Windows. This version also showed, as a preview, the new .NET MAUI (Muti-Platform App UI) – which will be covered ahead as it is included in .Net 7 – that makes possible to build native client apps for desktop and mobile OS with a single codebase (kind of a cooler upgraded version of and MVC simplifying multi-platform development).

And finally in February 2022 it was released Preview 1 of .Net 7

(https://devblogs.microsoft.com/dotnet/asp-net-core-updates-in-net-7-preview-1/), which is to be launched in November this year. In the next chapter it will be covered more thoroughly but the planned areas of focus on .Net 7 are: Performance, HTTP/3, Minimal APIs, SignalR, Razor, Blazor, gRPC, MVC and Orleans. Since then, much more information was released and we will go through it in the following chapters.

Figure 1.1: .Net 7
Image downloaded from .Net blog

Examples of .Net 6

As seen earlier, .Net 6 implemented a few changes and updates.

Below will be some code samples from earlier versions *versus* .Net 6 (*although I will be introducing .Net 7, it is still important to know some upgrades made on .Net 6*).

I will give some examples of code made on earlier versions and the code that is now created and done in .Net 6. It will cover only some topics as this is just to understand what Microsoft is been working on and to show that everything is getting simpler and easier to work on these new versions.

Middleware integration

Middleware is something that sits between the requestor and the target and directly modify the response, log information, or modify the behaviour of code that generates the response. It can be used, for example, for logging requests.

In earlier versions it was used a Startup File, like the following code sample:

```
1.  public class Startup
2.  {
```

```
3.     public void Configur(IApplicationBuilder app=
4.     {
5.         app.UseStaticFiles();
6.     }
7. }
```

Since .Net 6 there is no need of this file and class, being all inserted directly without classes or namespaces in the program file:

```
1. var builder = WebApplication.CreateBuilder(args);
2. var app = builder.Build();
3.
4. app.UseStaticFiles();
5.
6. app.Run();
```

Routing

Routing is responsible for matching incoming HTTP requests and dispatching those requests to the endpoints. An application can have routing configured using Controllers, Razor Pages, SignalR, gRPC Services, Endpoint enabled middleware or delegates and lambdas that are registered with routing.

In earlier versions there was the need to call **UseEndpoints** or **UseRouting**:

```
1.  public class Startup
2.  {
3.      public void Configure(IApplicationBuilder app)
4.      {
5.          app.UseRouting();
6.          app.UseEndpoints(endpoints =>
7.          {
8.              endpoints.MapRazorPages();
9.              endpoints.MapDefaultControllerRoute();
10.         });
11.
12.     }
13. }
```

Now, it is not used anymore, and can be done directly:

```
1. var builder = WebApplication.CreateBuilder(args);
2. var app = builder.Build();
3.
4. app.MapRazorPages();
5. app.MapDefaultControllerRoute();
6.
7. app.Run();
```

Add Services

To add memory cache services, custom scoped services, or other type of services you have to use Dependency Injection which allows an Inversion of Control between classes and their dependencies.

As in the previous examples, it was needed to use Startup and create a Configuration Method and call the services on it:

```
 1. public class Startup
 2. {
 3.    public void ConfigureServices(IServiceCollection services)
 4.    {
 5.        //Add Memory Cache Services
 6.        services.AddMemoryCache();
 7.
 8.        //Add Custom Scoped Services
 9.        services.AddScoped<ITestService, TestService>();
10.        services.AddScoped<ITestRepository, TestRepository>();
11.    }
12. }
```

Now, it is much simpler:

```
1.  var builder = WebApplication.CreateBuilder(args);
2.  //Add Memory Cache Services
3.  builder.Services.AddMemoryCache();
4.  //Add Custom Scoped Services
5.  builder.Services.
    AddScoped<ITestService,TestService>();
6.  builder.Services.AddScoped<ITestRepository,
    TestRepository>();
7.
8.  var app = builder.Build();
```

So, summarizing, one of the changes that can be seen more effectively was "removing" the need to use a Startup page and now you can add all your calls and iterations in a simpler and direct way, in **Program.cs**, without the need of creating any classes, also.

Conclusion

After this chapter we are now aware a bit more about .Net and history of these technology and framework. We have also learned that this year is an historic landmark for Microsoft and .Net as it is, its 20th birthday!

It will be celebrated then, with many events, and with the launch in next November, of the version that brought us here and the one we will be discovering a bit further in following chapters: .Net 7.

So, sit tight and let's enjoy this ride and learn a little more about programming and about .Net and all its great functionalities. It is a great world and can help us a lot in our daily development tasks.

Hope you all enjoy this journey!

In the next chapter we will learn about .Net 7 features and libraries and also some comparison between .Net 6 and .Net 7.+

Join our book's Discord space

Join the book's Discord Workspace for Latest updates, Offers, Tech happenings around the world, New Release and Sessions with the Authors:

https://discord.bpbonline.com

CHAPTER 2
New Features and Libraries

Introduction

In the first chapter we have learned a bit of **.Net** story now it is the time to focus on **.Net 7** and analyse the new features and libraries it will include.

To do the same, we will check what Microsoft has been launching throughout these latest months with what will be included in this latest version and share some examples using Microsoft Dev Pages and comparing with **.Net 6.**

So, for this version, Microsoft will keep on working on the same basis that was used for .Net 6 and will continue to simplify the development experience, turning it in a more productive and unified platform.

.Net 7 will then have its major improvements being done in the following topics:

- Modern Client Development: .Net MAUI
- Cloud Native & Containers
- Upgrading existing .Net Apps

- JWT Authentication Improvements & Automation Configuration This version of .Net will also include a new version of C#, C#11.

It will also include performance improvements to make it faster and more efficient and improve some of the features that were presented on .Net 6, like Minimal **Application Programming Interface(APIs)** and Blazor. Also, Json will include a few improvements, mainly on the serialization options.

Structure

In this chapter we will discuss following topics:

- New features of this framework
- New libraries
- Comparison and examples between .Net 6 and .Net 7

New features of this framework

.Net 7 will arrive soon and will bring a series of improvements, to ease up and simplify all our programming jobs.

It will contain some improvements on features already implemented in the previous versions, but also will include some new and fresh additions.

Speaking of the improvements on already introduced features, we will go through some of them (information obtained from **https://betterprogramming.pub/6-worthy-features-in-net-7-for-anyweb-developer-6ac42b20426b**):

Blazor

Blazor was first introduced in .Net 3, 2018 version and is now being made desktop-ready, improving performance, accessibility, and security, and adding the possibility to consider

different screen resolutions. Although further will dedicate a chapter to this feature ahead, and will go through some of the new features that will be included in .Net 7 (based on information taken from Microsoft DevBlogs: **https://devblogs.microsoft.com/dotnet/asp-net-core-updates-in-dotnet-7-preview-7/**).

Figure 2.1: .*Blazor Logo*

New loading page

The Blazor WebAssemply will include a new loading **User Interface** (**UI**) that shows the progress of loading the app. It is implemented with HTML and CSS in Blazor WebAssembly template introducing new CSS custom properties provided by Blazor WebAssembly:

- **--blazor-load-percentage**: The percentage of app files loaded
- **--blazor-load-percentage-text**: Represents the percentage of loaded files, from app, with a round to the nearest whole number

With this, you can build a customized loading UI that matches the style of your own Blazor WebAssembly apps.

Data binding modifiers

Blazor allows to powerfully make data binding between Elements from the UI or component parameters and .Net objects. In .Net 7, Microsoft introduces new modifiers: **@bind:after**, **@bind:get**, **@bind:set**.

The first modifier (after) allows us to run async logic in an easier way. For example, the **SearchDates** async method will run automatically after the date in **dateField** is changed:

```
1.   <input @bind="dateField" @bind:after="SearchDates" />
2.
3.   @code {
4.             DateTime.dateField;
5.
6.             async Task SearchDates()
```

```
 7.     {
 8.                    //perform search in some data us-
        ing the date in the dateField
 9.     }
10. }
```

The other two modifiers (get and set), which are always used together will allow us to simplify the update of a component parameter value when an underlying UI element is changed. For example:

```
1. <input @bind:get="MyDate" @bind:set="DateChanged" />
2.
3. @code {
4.    [Parameter] public DateTime MyValue {get; set;}
5.    [Parameter] public EventCallback<DateTime> DateChanged {get; set;}
```

Virtualization improvements

Another improvement expected for Blazor will be on the use of **Virtualize** component that renders a spacer element, that will be used to specify what will be the vertical height of the area that will be scrollable. It uses a **div** with the height defined.

But, in some cases, the parent element might not allow child **div** elements. In these cases, now it can be used the new **SpacerElement** parameter to configure the spacer element that **Virtualize** uses:

```
1. <Virtualize SpacerElement="tr">...</Virtualize>
```

Navigation manager

In this version, Blazor will allow to pass states when navigating, using **NavigationManager**.

This mechanism allows a communication between different pages that will be simpler than it is now. You can push the state you want to the browser's history stack, so it can be accessed later using these properties when listening for location changed events:

NavigationManager.HistoryEntryState or
LocationChangedEventArgs.HistoryEntryState.

Additional cryptography support

.Net 7 enables more cryptographic algorithms by taking advantage of `SubtleCrypto` when possible. In the first previews of this version, other than supporting the SHA family algorithms (SHA1, SHA256, SHA384, SHA512), it will also support HMACSHA1, HMACSHA256, HMACSHA384, HMACSHA512, AES (only CBC mode), Rfc28958DeriveBytes (PBKDF2) and HKDF.

New problem details service

.Net 7 will introduce a new problem details service based on the `IProblemDetailsService` interface for generating problem details responses in our apps.

We can add problem details service using the following code:

```
builder.Services.AddProblemDetails();
```

Afterwards, it is possible to write a problem details response from any layer by simply calling `IProblemDetailsService.WriteAsync`.

The response can also be customized using `ProblemDetailsOptions`. And, if you want, you can create your own `IProblemDetailsWriter` implementation for advanced customizations, always remembering that these implementations must be registered before the call to the `AddProblemDetails` method.

Diagnostics middleware updates

Another update and improvement made on this .Net version was made on middleware, so they can generate problem details HTTP responses when the new `IProblemsDetailsService` is registered.

The diagnostics middleware, which was updated to generate problem details, were: `ExceptionHandlerMiddleware` (when a custom handler is not defined), `StatusCodePagesMiddleware` (by default), `DeveloperExceptionPageMiddleware` (when `text/html` is not accepted).

Minimal API

Minimal APIs were also introduced in the latest .Net 6 and allows to create lightweight simple APIs without the overhead of controllers.

They've got a few improvements in this new .Net 7. For example, it will contain support for endpoint filters, better support for bindings of query or header parameters and it will allow request bodies to be read as stream, optimizing file upload.

Also, the syntax will get some improvements and it will be possible to define routes as groups. A simplification in the authentication will be included, as well.

.Net 7 will contain the ability to group endpoints with a common route prefix, for example. It will also include the implementation of typed results by turning it public, and with it, simplifying type assertions during tests; improving OpenAPI so that it will be able to return, from minimal APIs, more than one result type.

Now, we will go through some of these improvements (based on information taken from Microsoft DevBlogs: **https://devblogs.microsoft.com/dotnet/asp-net-core-updates-in-dotnet-7-preview-4/**).

Typed results

In the previous .Net 6 version, it was introduced the `IResult` interface. This interface will represent minimal APIs return values that won't be implicitly supported, to serialize the returned object to HTTP response, using JSON.

This interface was then implemented using a static `Result` class to create objects that will represent different types of responses, just by defining what status code will be handed by the response, to redirect to another URL.

As this was created as internal, it was difficult to implement and to use, so in .Net 7, the types that implement `IResult` have been made public, simplifying type assertions when testing.

Besides this, it will be introduced a new `Microsoft.AspNetCore.Http.TypedResults` static class. This class is the new version of the existing `Microsoft.AspNetCore.Http.Results` class. It can be used in the minimal APIs to create instances of `IResult`, implementing types and preserving concrete type information.

OpenAPI improvements

Another improvement made will be the support for **Microsoft. AspNetCore.OpenApi** package, which will allow APIs to interact with the OpenAPI specification in minimal APIs. (*Just a quick reminder that OpenAPI specification provides a cross-language, i.e., independent of the language, standard for describing RESTful APIs*).

This new support will include package references, for applications that enable the use of minimal API, created using a template with **--enable-openapi** and will also expose a **WithOpenApi** extension method that will be able to generate an **OpenApiOperation** which will derive from an existing endpoint's route handler and metadata.

Next is shown an example on how to call **WithOpenApi**.:

```
1. app.MapGet("/todos/{id}", (int id) => ...)
2.    .WithOpenApi();
```

Also, we can have an overload extension method, as shown in the next example:

```
1. app.MapGet("/todos/{id}", (int id) => ...)
2.    .WithOpenApi(operation => {
3.        operation.Summary = "Retrieve a Todo given its ID";
4.        operation.Parameters[0].AllowEmptyValue = false;
5.        return operation;
6.    });
```

Self-describing minimal APIs

Minimal APIs allows the framework to use type information as part of our application's route handlers, in addition to implicit behaviour of the framework, thus documenting OpenAPI/Swagger APIs details.

In .Net 7, Microsoft added two interfaces to ASP.Net Core that will allow minimal API types to be used not only in route handlers but also in endpoint metadata: **IEndpointMetadataProvider** and **IEndpointParameterMetadataProvider**. These interfaces will use a new feature (using the new C#11): static abstract interface members which will declare static methods. When the endpoint is built and if these methods are present on route handler return types or parameters, the framework will then be able to call them. Here's a sample, from Microsoft, on how the interfaces will look like:

```
1. namespace Microsoft.AspNetCore.Http.Metadata;
2.
3. public interface IEndpointMetadataProvider
4. {
5.     static abstract void PopulateMetadata(EndpointMetadataContext context);
6. }
7.
8. public interface IEndpointParameterMetadataProvider
9. {
10.    static abstract void PopulateMetadata(EndpointParameterMetadataContext parameterContext);
11. }
```

IEndpointMetadataProvider can be implemented by types returned from a route handler or accepted by a route hander as a parameter.

IEndpointParameterMetadataProvider can be implemented only by types accepted by a route hander as a parameter and will have the **ParameterInfo** for the associated route handler parameter when called.

Return multiple result types

Microsoft introduces new **Results<TResult1, TResult2, TResultN>** generic union types, together with **TypesResults** class, allowing that a route handler can return multiple **IResult-**

implementing specific types, and each of those types that implement.

IEndpointMetadataProvider, will be included in the endpoint's metadata, updating the automatically description that the various HTTP results will have for APIs in OpenAPI/Swagger.

This union types, that are specified in generic arguments, will be converted to an instance of themselves automatically by the compiler. This will improve the compile-time, by providing it the ability to check that a route handler only returns the result that it declares.

MVC

MVC, besides the classic **Model View Controller (MVC)** approach, and Razor Pages, will have Minimal API added to the model binding.

These binding will ensure that parameters of the action methods are filled with values, instead of being bound via request body (complex types) and route or query string (simple types).

The use of Minimal API in MVC will allow the binding of complex types via dependency injection container and, if they are registered as a service, they can be passed to the action method. This improvement will also be available for controllers and razor pages, in the future.

It will be possible to inject services into the action metho, being no longer necessary to inject it exclusively into the controller's constructor.

A new TryParse model binder is now available, allowing to bind all types that implement a TryParse method.

Links

Also, link generation and routing are one of the things Microsoft chose to innovate and change in this version.

The principal point will be to try to make link generation more type-safe, passing a generic variant, instead of the controller's name and action name as string. The feature was not implemented yet but the API suggestions from Microsoft look quite nice, as in the following sample code:

```
1. // Url that contains some action in a controller:
2. Url.Action<ControllerA>(c => c.Index());
3.
4. // Url linkiing to an action inside the same
   controller
5. Url.Action(c => c.Index());
```

New libraries

Microsoft will make some changes and improvements in lots of elements, including libraries.

.Net 7 will have new features and, as it focuses on better performance and simplicity of use, it will also contain some adaptations and improvements made on libraries.

Nullable annotations for Microsoft.Extensions

One of the first improvements that was released, was the annotation for nullability which is now included (as of Preview 1), in the following libraries:

`Microsoft.Extensions.DependencyInjection.Abstractions`

`Microsoft.Extensions.Logging.Abstractions`

`Microsoft.Extensions.Primitives`

`Microsoft.Extensions.FileSystemGlobbing`

`Microsoft.Extensions.DependencyModel`

`Microsoft.Extensions.Configuration.Abstractions`

`Microsoft.Extensions.FileProviders.Abstractions`

`Microsoft.Extensions.FileProviders.Physical`

`Microsoft.Extensions.Configuration.Binder`

`Microsoft.Extensions.Configuration.CommandLine`

`Microsoft.Extensions.Configuration.EnvironmentVariables`

`Microsoft.Extensions.Configuration.FileExtensions`

`Microsoft.Extensions.Configuration.Ini`

`Microsoft.Extensions.Configuration.Json`

The plan is to have all **Microsoft.Extensions** libraries annotated for nullability, by the time of the release of .Net 7.

System.Text.RegularExpressions improvements and new APIs

Microsoft keeps launching new previews and new information about the changes and improvements that will be made in .Net 7.

On Preview 4 it was added new APIs to add span support into Regex library. These changes will impact on improving extensibility point for better performance and span-based matching, including more functionalities to a free allocation **Regex.Enumerate**, improve Regex's way of managing **RegexOptions.IgnoreCase**.

The main span-based APIs that are added in this preview will be:

- **Regex.IsMatch(ReadOnlySpan<char> input)**: Used to indicate if a regular expression and an input span will match.

- **Regex.Count(ReadOnlySpan<char> input)**: Identifies and returns how many occurrences of a regular expression exists in an input string.

- **Regex.EnumerateMatches(ReadOnlySpan<char> input)**: Enumerate, by returning a **ValueMatchEnumerator**, how many occurrences of a regular expression exists in an input span, iterating though all the matches found.

Also, for Regex, Microsoft enhanced its performance and improved Regex source generated code. As far as performance improvements they focus on handling some of the more commonly used and popular Regex sets, by finding possible positions when a match exists, using spans for some internal types, avoiding allocations – if possible – an, with it, speeding up the engine, logic for when a loop can be made atomic.

LibraryImportGenerator

On preview 7 of .Net 7, Microsoft showed **LibraryImport** source generator, which is now available to all users.

This source generator is designed to be a replacement for the majority of **DllImport** uses, in the runtime product and user code. All .Net Libraries have adopted **LibraryImport** and have been shipping with source generated marshalling code since preview 1 of this .Net version.

To benefit from this source generated marshalling, usages of **DllImport** with **LibraryImport**. So, let us check the differences between then and now:Then:

```
1. public static class Native
2. {
3.     [DllImport(nameof(Native).CharSet=Chasert.Unicode)]
4.     public extern static string ToLower(string str);
5. }
```

Now:

```
1. public static class Native
2. {
3.     [LibraryImport(nameof(Native).StringMarshalling= StringMarshalling.Utf16)]
4.     public static partial string ToLower(string str);
5. }
```

.Net 6 vs .Net 7

Let us now take a lot at some differences and improvements, marking some of the differences that .Net 7 will have regarding his older sibling .Net 6.

As seen before, .Net 6 introduced some productivity improvements and some new features like Blazor, .Net MAUI, Json, and minimal APIs. These improvements and features are now being upgraded and updated in .Net 7 and this is what we will see next.

Blazor and .Net MAUI

Blazor is a framework that can run the application view on the client side – and then sending the browser the HTML. In fact, the name Blazor comes from the union of Browser and Razor (which is the .Net HTML view generation engine) and was first implemented in .Net 6.

.Net MAUI is the new framework that Microsoft is working on, since .Net 6, that will focus on mobile applications, eventually replacing Xamarin, or being its evolution.

But, with .Net 7, Microsoft is willing to go further here and "join" these two frameworks, creating a Blazor Hybrid.

Blazor Hybrid will allow native apps to leverage web technologies like HTML and CSS for additional functionalities. A hybrid app might use an embedded Webview control to render Web UI while also leveraging native device capabilities, as can be read in **Visual Studio Magazine (VSM)**and seen in the following image:

Figure 2.2: .Native UI and Web UI

Cloud native and containers

Microsoft is trying to steer towards cloud native applications. So, to do that, there were some improvements made in .Net 7, that didn't appear in .Net 6:

- Making easier and simpler to setup and configure all the necessary things for the implementation of secure authentication and authorization.
- Enhancing application startup and runtime execution performance.

Also, there will be an investment in a new cross-platform framework designed for distributed applications – Orleans – that should bring some improvements to these developments.

And, as it has been their flag throughout all this process: simplify and improve the developer experience for containerized .Net applications is another thing that's in place for .Net 7.

Json

Json is a well-known and hugely used format, not only in .Net 6 but in previews versions.

Although, Microsoft wanted to enhance and twerk it a bit, introducing a new

JsonSerializerOptions, including a **JsonWriterOptions**. **MaxDeph** property – and verifying that this value is derived from the corresponding, and adding **Patch** methods to **System.Net.Http. Json**.

So, thanks to these additions it will now be possible to serialize and deserialize polymorphic type hierarchies.

The next example, taken from **Microsoft devblogs**, shows how this will work:

```
1. [JsonDerivedType(typeof(Derived))]
2. public class Base
3. {
4.     public int X { get; set; }
5. }
6.
7. public class Derived : Base
8. {
9.     public int Y { get; set; }
10. }
11.
12. //.NET 7 Serialization
13. Base value = new Derived();
14. JsonSerializer.Serialize<Base>(value); // { "X" : 0,
    "Y" : 0 }
15.
16. //.NET 7 Deserialization
17. Base value = JsonSerializer.Deserialize<Base>(@"{
    ""X"" : 0, ""Y"" : 0 }
");
18. value is Derived; // false
```

JWT authentication configuration

In .Net 7 preview 5, Microsoft announced great improvements for JWT Authentication Configuration.

Before .Net 7, configuring JWT in ASP.Net Core projects was one of the hardest parts of writing APIs and one of the main complaints made from developers. It required many steps including adding middleware at startup process and configuring services.

So, brace yourselves! Now, in .Net 7, it will be much simpler to configure JWT.

It can now be configured automatically directly from the configuration system, due to the addition of a default configuration section when configuring with the new Authentication property on **WebApplicationBuilder**.

```
1. var builder = WebApplication.CreateBuilder(args);
2.
3. builder.Authentication.AddJwtBearer(); // New property
4.
5. var app = builder.Build();
```

These steps will automatically add required middleware in a same way that **WebApplicationBuilder** does for routing.

But it is not all. Individual authentication schemes will set options parameters from **appsettings.json** automatically, which will help to configure parameters between all the environments. **Appsettings.json** will look like this, now:

```
1. {
2.    "Logging": {
3.       "LogLevel": {
4.          "Default": "Information",
5.          "Microsoft.AspNetCore": "Warning"
6.       }
7.    },
8.    "AllowedHosts":"*",
```

```
 9.         "Authentication": {
10.             "DefaultScheme":"JwtBearer",
11.             "Schemes": {
12.                 "JwtBearer": {
13.                     "Audiences": ["http://localhost:5000", "https://localhost:5001"],
14.                     "ClaimsIssuer": "user-jwt-here"
15.                 }
16.             }
17.         }
18. }
```

C# 11

Another improvement, which is also focused on performance (73,5% faster than the previous), and will be implemented in .Net 7, is the new C# 11.

It will contain some new features that didn't exist in C#10 which was present in .Net 6:

- **Generic attributes**

  Also, Generic attributes are now introduced in C# 11.

- **Required members**

  It will introduce a new modifier to fields and properties: **required**. This implies that constructors and callers will need to initialize values for properties and fields that have this modifier. So, it will be needed to introduce a new attribute on the constructor, to tell the compiler that all required members are initialized: **SetsRequiredMembers**.

- **Raw string literals**

  The use of raw string literals will allow the use of random text without the need to use text escaping. Its format must be, at the minimum 3 double quotes ("""..""").

- **UTF-8 string literals**

  Another literal introduced in C#11 is UTF-8, which will permit to convert UTF-8 characters, at compile time, to their byte representation.

- **List patterns**

    This feature will increase pattern matching, allowing it to now being able to match sequences of elements inside a list or an array. It can be used with properties, types, constants, relational patterns, and any other pattern.

- **Auto-default structs**

    Another improvement is to initialize properties or fields, that are not initialized by a constructor, setting default values in C#11 structs, using the compiler, which didn't happen on later versions.

- **Pattern match Span<char> on a constant string**

    C#11 will allow pattern matching, on a constant string, between a Span<char> and ReadOnlySpan<char>.

- **Extended nameof scope**

    The scope for **nameof** expressions will also be expanded, allowing us, on the parameter declaration or method, to specify the name of an attribute method parameter.

- **An unsigned right-shift operator**

    It will also contain a new right-shift operator >>> that moves bits right without replacing the high order but on each shift.

- **Numeric IntPtr**

    Another simplification is the use of **nint** and **nuint** types which serve as pseudonym to **System.IntPtr** and **System.UIntPtr** respectively.

- **Newlines in string interpolation expressions**

    This will allow any valid C# code that is written between { }, improving code readability. It will be quite interesting and helpful when using longer expressions, for example, LINQ queries or switch expressions.

- **Static abstract member in interfaces for generic math support**

    C# 11 will add static abstract members in interfaces to define them. This will include: other static members, overloadable operators, and static properties.

Conclusion

In this chapter we have gone through the new features and libraries of .Net 7 and have seen some differences between .Net versions 6 and 7.

Microsoft is still actively working on the development and are still showing some new features and some previews are being launched.

As we are advancing on our journey, we are understanding better all the benefits of working and knowing about .Net, and all the improvements that this new version will be bring to our daily work.

We learned in this chapter that Microsoft keeps improving the performance of .Net, enabling our programming jobs to be easier and simpler – and that is always a plus!

Microsoft also rectified to some "complaints" from us, developers, and corrected some issues, twerked some things and simplified others. This is always a good sign for the future as it means we are involved in the evolution of the platform, which will also allow us to improve our work and evolve – and make the world evolve with us!

In the next chapter we will go through what we've learned here and show how to design a simple first program, using .Net 7. Keep in your toes, we've got a lot to go through and the ride is only beginning!

Join our book's Discord space

Join the book's Discord Workspace for Latest updates, Offers, Tech happenings around the world, New Release and Sessions with the Authors:

https://discord.bpbonline.com

CHAPTER 3
Writing Your First .Net 7 Program

Introduction

Now we have gathered some history of .Net and know some of the features and libraries that will be presented in .Net 7, being also able to recognize some of the differences between this version and the latest .Net 6, it is time to begin writing a simple small program, using .Net 7.

First, we will start showing how to create a solution, then adding the project and the pages, and implementing this project which is running it.

Also, we will explore some features that are new or newly refreshed in .Net 7.

For this, it will be used the IDE Visual Studio 2022 and the pages will be created in a simple way using Razor.

Structure

So, the topics that will be covered in this chapter will be:

- Creating .Net 7 project \ solution

- Adding the pages
- Implementing the simple project

Creating a .Net 7 project\solution

Let us now proceed with our adventure, and continue in learning how to create a project and solution in .Net 7.

Roll up your sleeves and start.

To do so, – being version 7 or older – we will use an IDE, and, for me, Visual Studio has always been the best choice.

If you do not have it, download and install Visual Studio 2022 (For example: Enterprise or Community versions). You may also download the latest version available of .Net 7 SDK.

Now, that you are up and running, let us proceed with the following steps.

1. Open Visual Studio 2022 and click **Create a New Project**, like it is shown on *Figure 3.1*:

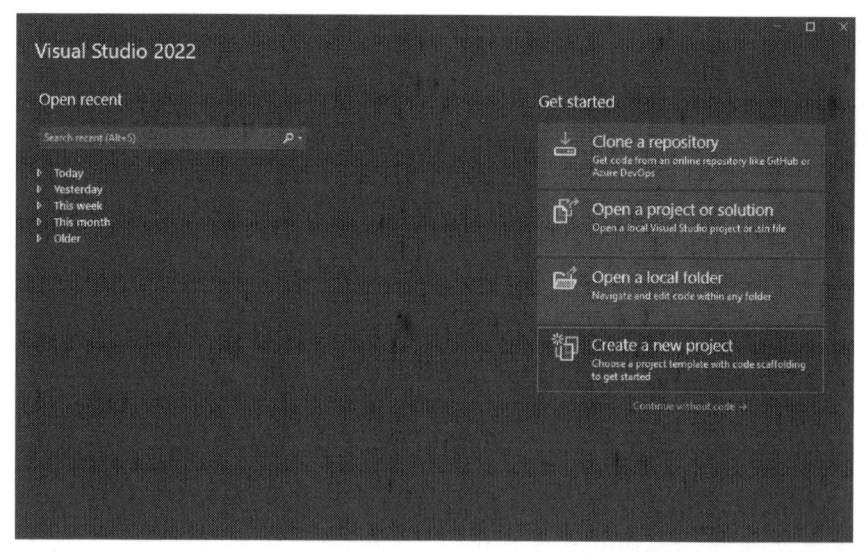

Figure 3.1: Open Visual Studio and Create a New Project

2. From the project types list, select the one we will be using, for example, ASP.Net Core WebApp - You can select, in the dropdown list "**All Languages**" C#, in "**All Platforms**" Windows,

Writing Your First .Net 7 Program ■ 29

and in "**All Project Types**" Web. This will filter the projects available - , like the example shown in the next figure:

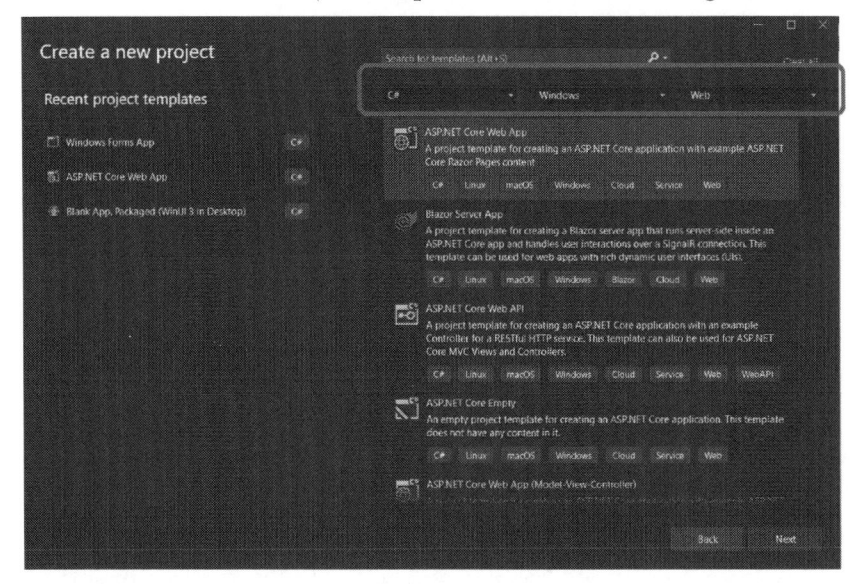

Figure 3.2: Select Project Type

3. Then provide a name to the project and solution as well as a location, as seen in *Figure 3.3*:

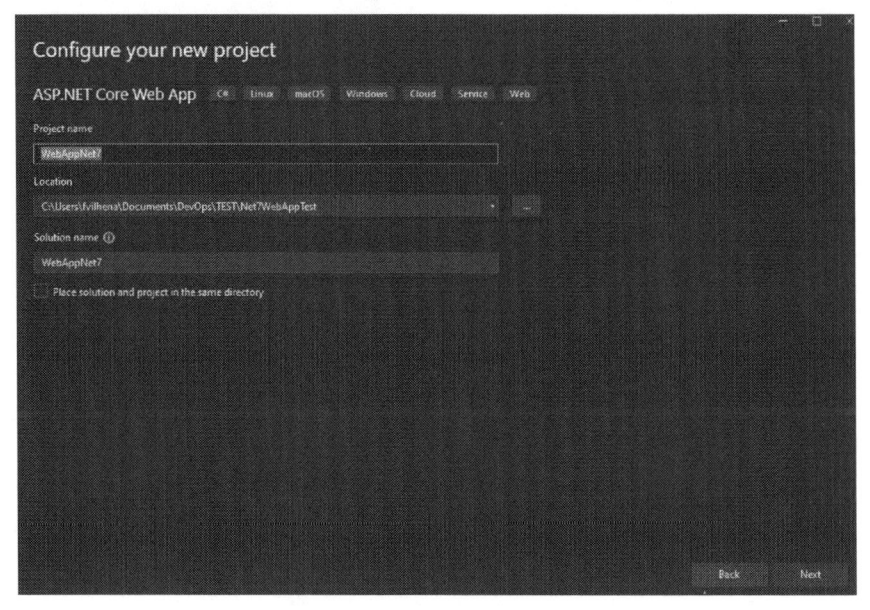

Figure 3.3: Give a Name and Location for Solution and Project

30 ■ .NET 7 for Jobseekers

4. Select the framework .Net 7.0 (Preview) and click **Create**. In case you don't see .Net 7.0 in the list, you must first download it from Microsoft. You will see something similar to which is depicted in the following *Figure 3.4:*

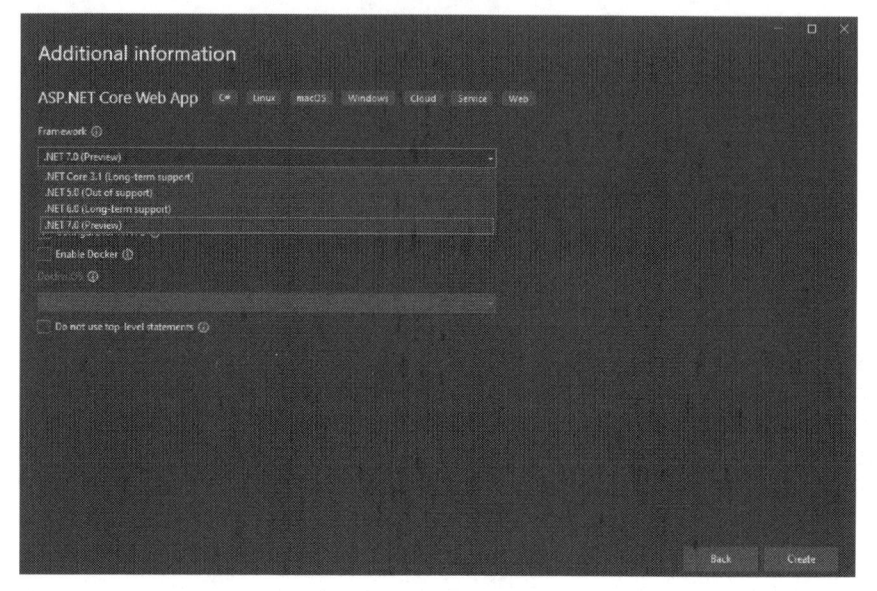

Figure 3.4: *Select the framework and create the project\solution*

Now, the project and solution are created as can be seen in *Figure 3.5:*

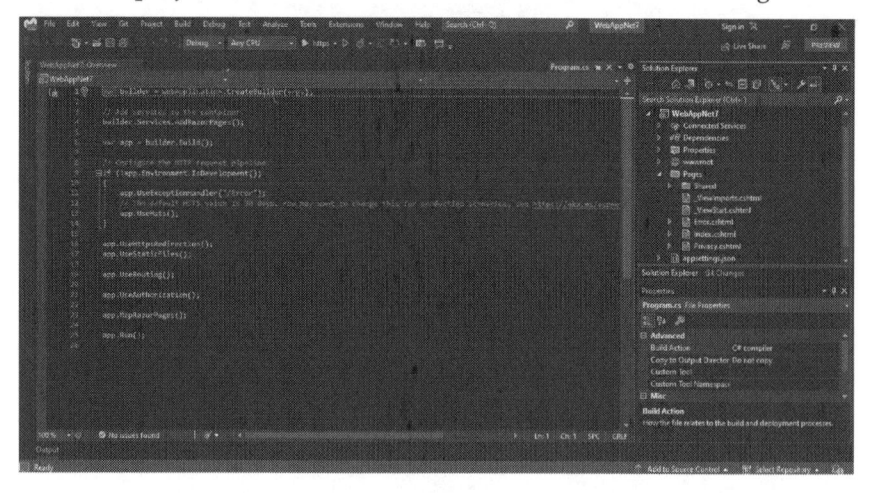

Figure 3.5: *View of Program.cs after the creation of the project\solution*

Writing Your First .Net 7 Program ■ 31

5. The `csproj` file looks like the following figure:

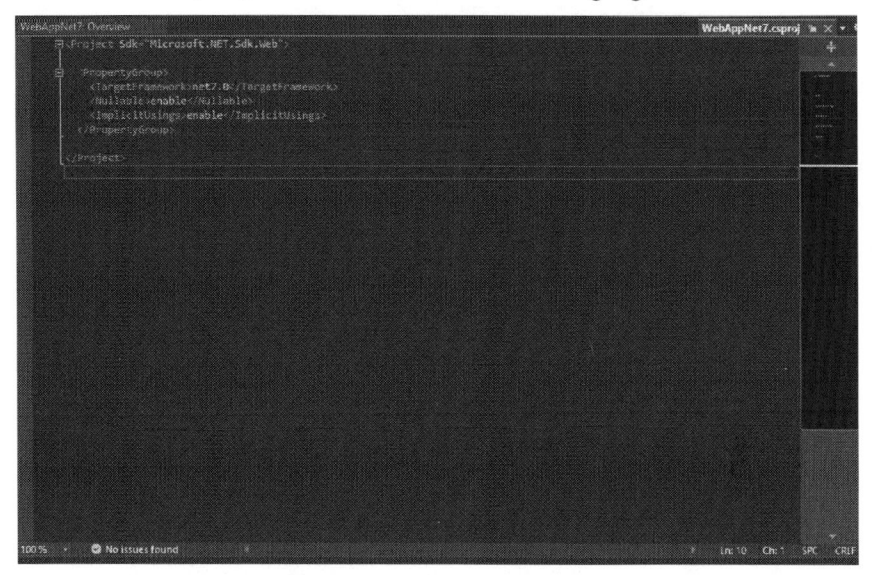

Figure 3.6: View of .csproj file after the creation of the project\solution

To open `.csproj`, if it fails to open on its own, you can access it in Solution Explorer – it is the one, in our example, called WebAppNet7, right under the Solution. Solution Explorer will also have a set of folders that show you the separated parts of your project, as shown in the following figure:

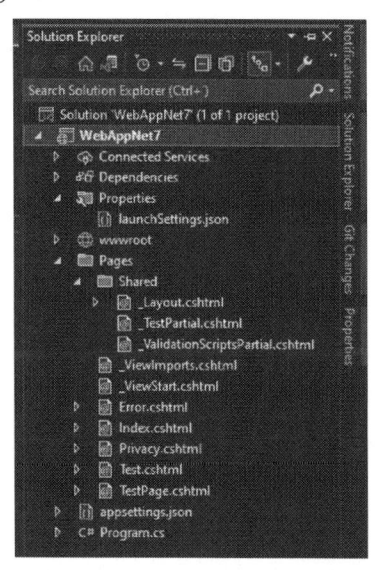

Figure 3.7: Solution Explorer and WebAppNet7.csproj

We can also change the framework and C# version. We need to add in the **.csproj** file, the following code lines (for release and debug), if we want our project to be in C#10, for example:

```
1. <PropertyGroup Condition="'$(Configuration)|$(Plat-
   form)' == 'Release|AnyCPU'">
2.     <LangVersion>10.0</LangVersion>
3. </PropertyGroup>
4.
5. <PropertyGroup Condition="'$(Configuration)|$(Plat-
   form)' == 'Debug|AnyCPU'">
6.     <LangVersion>10.0</LangVersion>
7. </PropertyGroup>
```

6. Now, if we execute the project, by pressing *F5* key, we will have a simple page like the following figure:

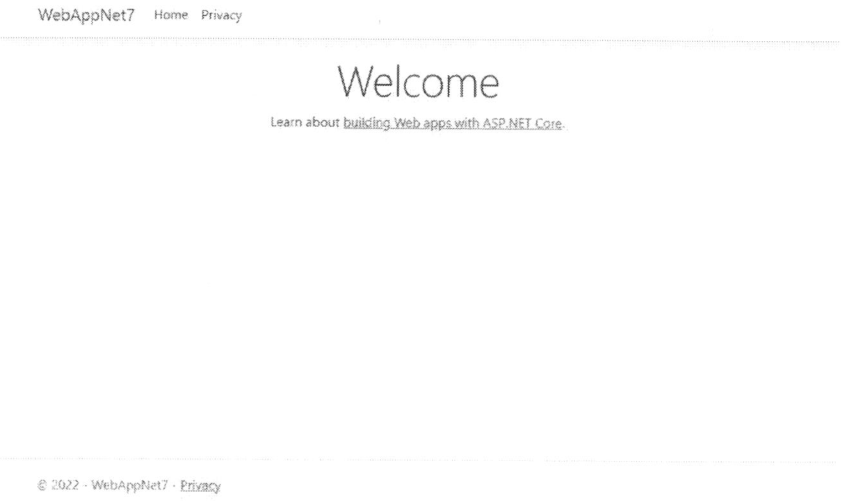

WebAppNet7 Home Privacy

Welcome
Learn about building Web apps with ASP.NET Core.

© 2022 - WebAppNet7 - Privacy

Figure 3.8: *Simple Home Page for our .Net Core Project\Solution using .Net 7*

7. So, to summarize, in this first point we were able to create a simple project\solution with .Net 7, using our Visual Studio IDE, for a Web Application, with Razor Pages.

8. Now, on the next point we will learn how to add more pages and interact between them.

Adding and configuring pages

Now, that we have seen how to create a simple project and solution, using .Net 7, is time to see how the pages are built and to make some changes and add some interactions between the pages.

So, on the solution explorer, select the **Index.cshtml** file and view the code, as in *Figure 3.9*:

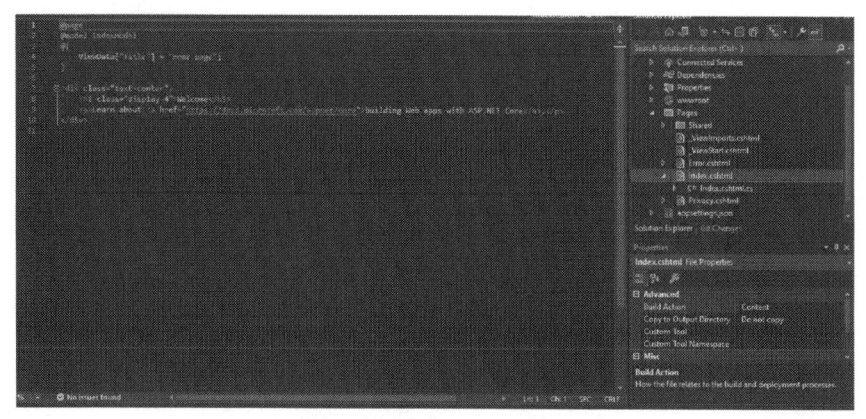

Figure 3.9: *View of the .cshtml page*

Each **.cshtml** file contains a .cs file associated, where the code behind is written. In our sample project let us navigate to **Index.cshtml.cs**. We will see something like shown in *Figure 3.10*:

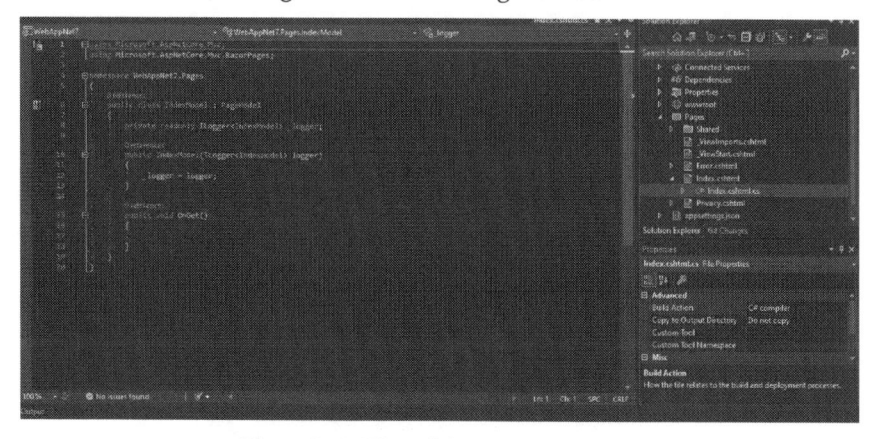

Figure 3.10: *View of the .cs code behind file*

Changing view Index.cshtml

Now that we have navigated through the pages, make a simple change on the view. For example, just change the Welcome phrase to something different like "**Enter .Net 7 Universe**".

1. `<div class="text-center">`
2. `<h1 class="display-4">Enter .Net 7 Universe </h1>`
3. `<p>Learn about <a href="https://docs.microsoft.com/aspnet/core">building Web apps with ASP.NET core</a>.</p>`
4. `</div>`

To do so, you must open again the **.cshtml** file and replace the display text to the one we want, as seen in the following figures.

First, we need to check the code to be replaced which is illustrated in *Figure 3.11*:

Figure 3.11: Code to be replaced, highlighted

Then, lets replace the code with our new line(s) of code as illustrated in *Figure 3.12*:

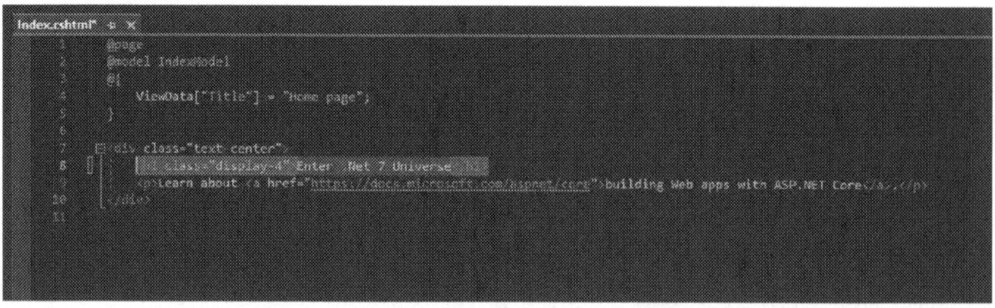

Figure 3.12: Replaced code, highlighted

So, after making this change, let us run our application and see how it is now:

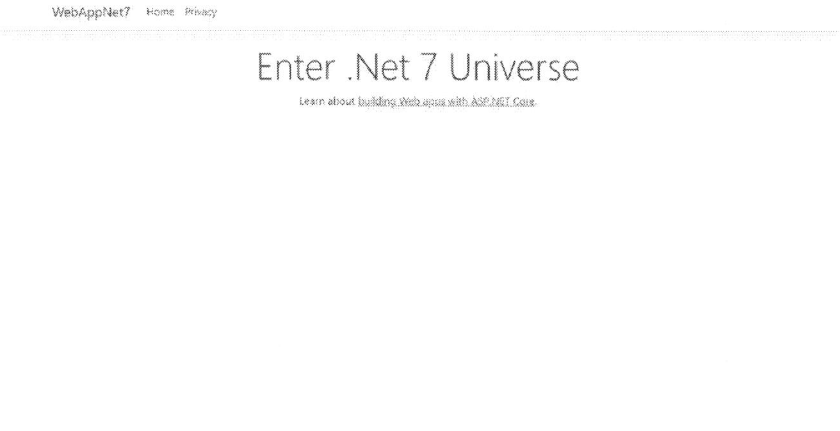

Figure 3.13: *New Home Page*

As we have seen it is easy to change and configure a simple page that we want to use in our application developed in .Net 7.

So, keep looking at the solution, the pages and how they interact.

Navigate through the Solution Explorer

Navigating in the solution, we will find the project, a **Pages** folder, with a **Shared** subfolder – that typically contains a Layout page and some Partial Pages that are shared by the other pages. We can also see a **wwwroot** folder that contains subfolders with `css, js and lib` (libraries used). Another important point is the **appsettings.json** where we can define, for example, the database connection for the project. And something that is different from previous versions of .Net: we now don't have **Startup** file, but only a **Program.cs** file, containing all the dependencies and injections (you can learn more about this in **https://learn.microsoft.com/en-us/dotnet/core/**

extensions/dependency-injection) needed. In the following *figure (3.14)* we can see this listing:

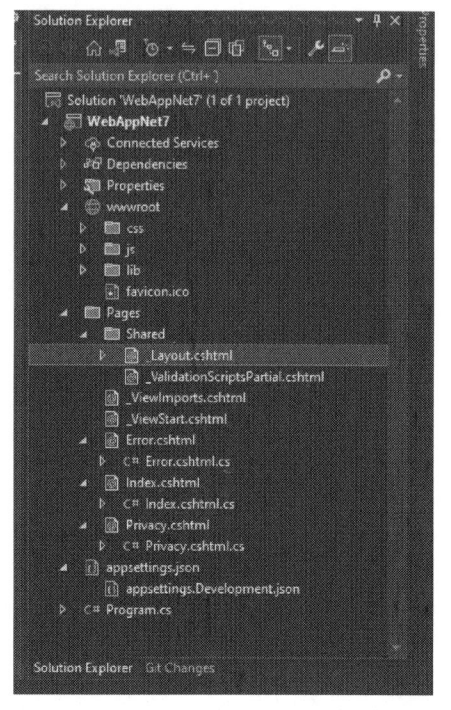

Figure 3.14: Solution Explorer with all the folders and files

Use minimal APIs

Now let us try something different. As we have seen before .Net 7 brings us minimal APIs, which help us to create HTTP APIs with minimal dependencies, and are perfect for microservices and applications that need to be simple and only include the minimum files, features, and dependencies. So, in our test project, let us experiment a bit and try to add a simple HTTP call to a basic homepage.

We will need to open **Program.cs** and include the following line:

```
1. app.MapGet("/", () => "Welcome to Minimal API .Net 7!");
```

Then we'll get something like it is shown in *Figure 3.15*:

Figure 3.15: Program.cs with minimal API call

Then, when we execute the application, instead of the homepage that we used to have, it will now be shown the following:

Figure 3.16: Minimal API result

Well, that was something different and quite interesting to see!

Add pages and interact between pages

But let us get back to the razor page and now try to interact between the pages.

As we can see there are two pages: **Index.cshtml** and **Privacy.cshtml**. Just for the fun of it, try to add another page to interact with the webapp.

On the **Solution Explorer**, go to **Pages**, right click on it and select **Add | Razor Page...** as shown in the figure:

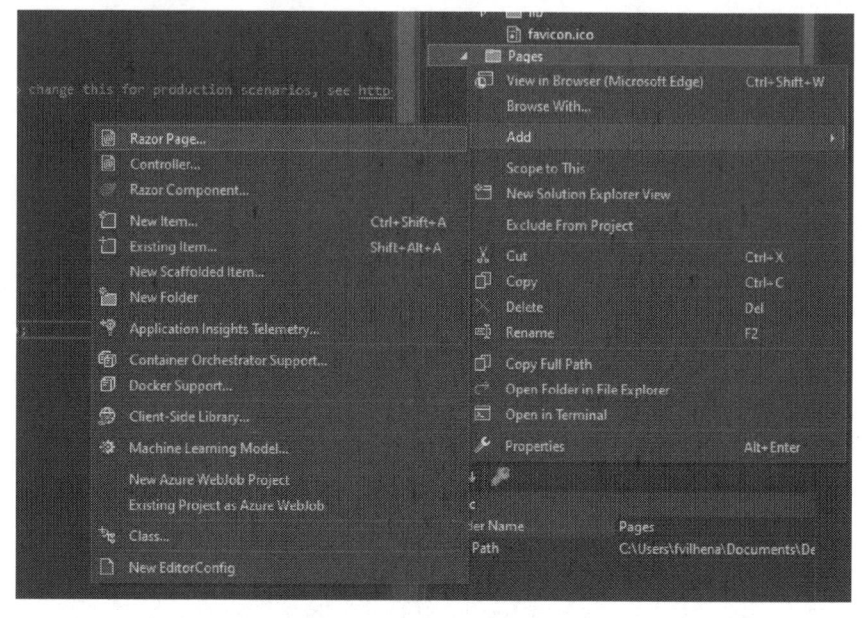

Figure 3.17: *Add new Razor Page*

This will open a popup as shown in *Figure 3.18*, and then select **Razor Page | Empty** and click on **Add**.

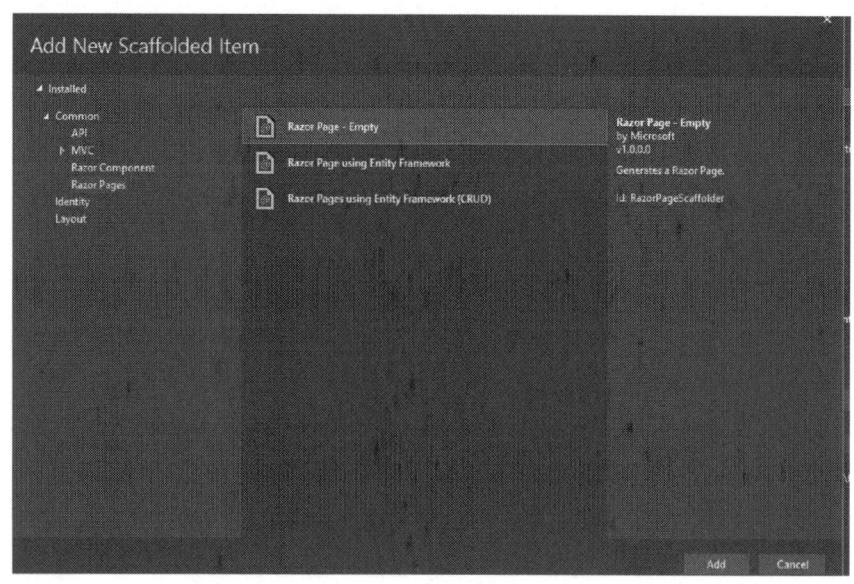

Figure 3.18: *Select the type of razor Page to Add*

Give the page a name and click, again on **Add**. In the following example, we will call it `Test.cshtml`.

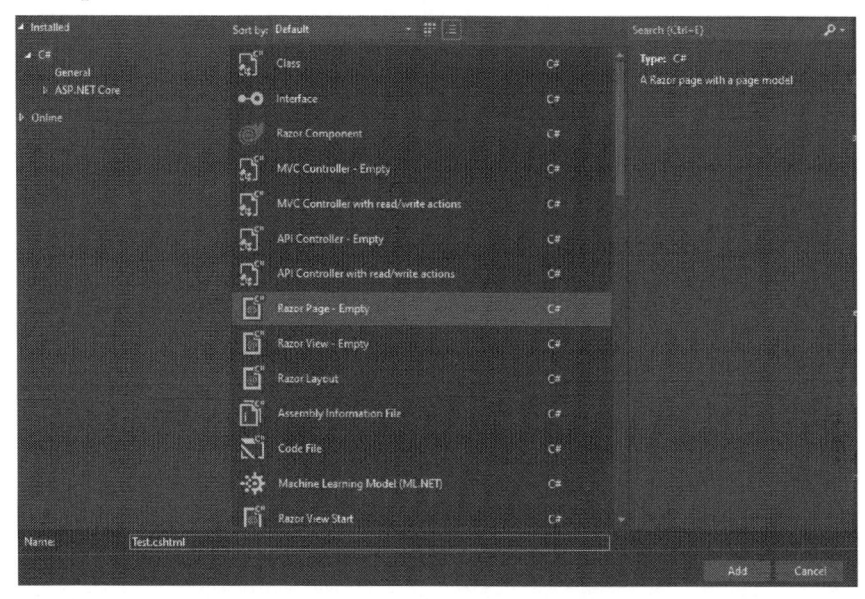

Figure 3.19: *Rename the page and add it to the project*

It will create an empty page, on which we will now work, as depicted in *Figure 3.20*:

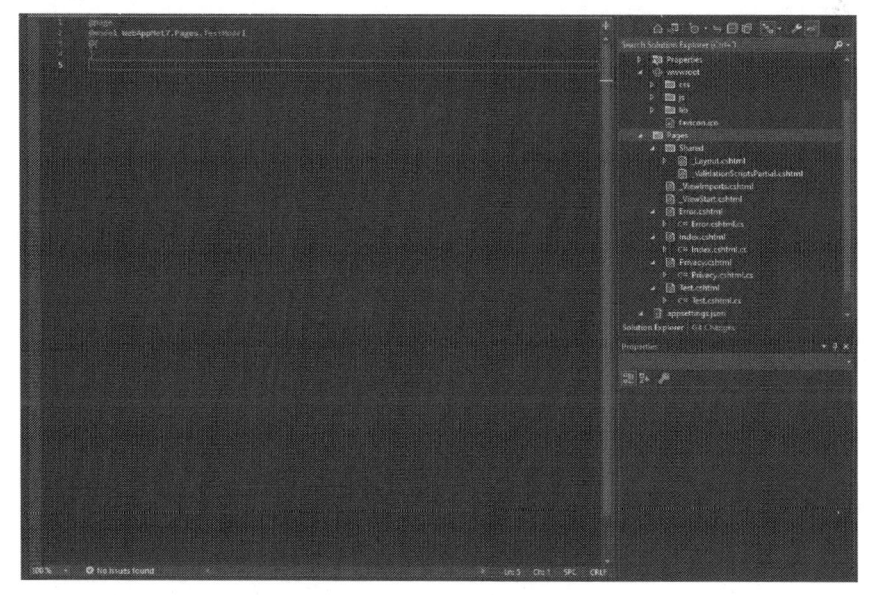

Figure 3.20: *Test.cshtml page*

So, let us now add some content to the page.

Start by inserting a title and a simple div with some text. Something like it is pictured in *Figure 3.21*:

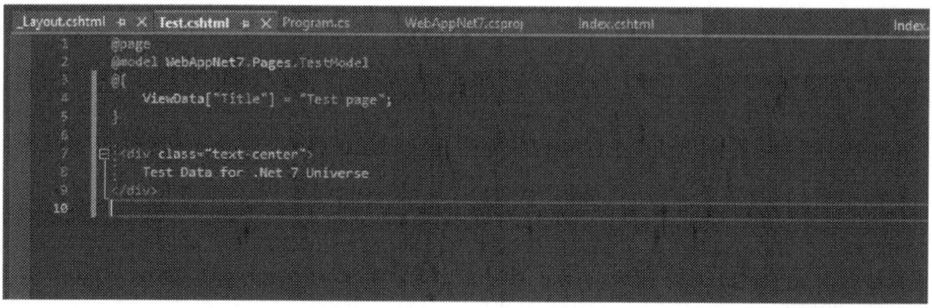

Figure 3.21: Add content to Test.cshtml page

Then, go to the code correspondent file (`Test.cshtml.cs`) and add a simple constructor with a logger, as it is done on the default pages, and as we can see in *Figure 3.22*:

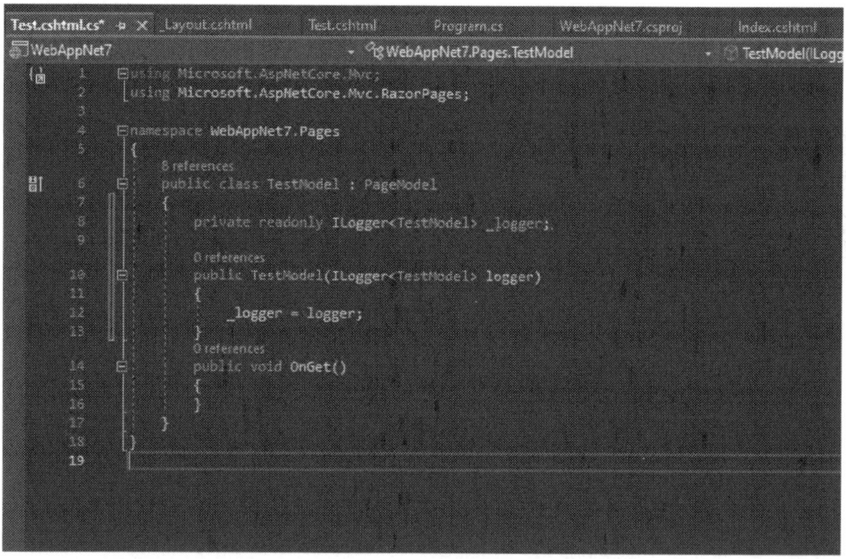

Figure 3.22: Add content to Test.cshtml.cs

Now, to test, we must add a link, in the layout page, to our test page, so that we can navigate there. It can be done, as shown in *Figure 3.23*:

Figure 3.23: Add link in Layout.cshtml

When executing the project, we will now see three menu options and we can navigate to our Test page, like it is shown in *Figure 3.24*:

Figure 3.24: View of Test page

Excellent! Now we know how to create a simple web page, to use minimal APIs and to insert and navigate to a Test page, using .Net 7.

That is great! Let us then proceed and see in the next point how to implement this project.

Implementing the project

To implement a .Net 7 project and solution we need to, as seen, create the solution and the project, add the pages, create the interactions between the pages and add all the connections that we need: for example, SMTP, database, file system connections, default data, and others.

To do that we can use **appsetting.json** to add all this connections, for example:

```
1.  {
2.     "App": {
3.        "Language": "pt",
4.        "SqlConn": "c:\\SQLConn\\Sql.json",
5.        "SqlError": true,
6.        "LogCalls": true,
7.        "LogError": true
8.     },
9.
10.    "FilePath": "C:\\MyFiles\\",
11.    "SMTP": {
12.       "SMTPServer": "mysmpt.domain.com",
13.       "EmailFrom": "myemail@domain.com"
14.    },
15.
16.    "Logging": {
17.       "LogLevel": {
18.          "Default": "Information",
19.          "Microsoft": "Warning"
20.       }
21.    },
22.
23.    "AllowedHosts": "*"
24.
25. }
```

We can also use, besides the Views, model files and controllers.

Models can contain database or classes definition. These models can now be used by the controllers to interact with the views, and, for example, get database data.

In *Figure 3.24* we can see a simple diagram on how these layers interact (Source: *Wikipedia*):

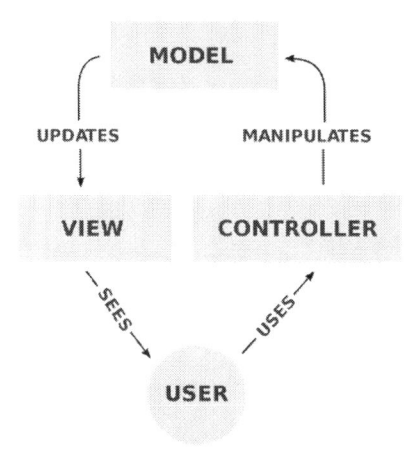

Figure 3.25: Model View Controller interaction

Ahead on this book, we will get back to this, by learning how to create the views, the controller, and the models to bind all our data.

But, for now, once we have all that we need, we can implement the project, by deploying it into an **Internet Information System (IIS)**, using Azure, for example.

After it is deployed, and thus implemented, we can access it from everywhere, inside or outside our domain, also depending on security issues.

Conclusion

In this chapter we have seen how to create a simple project and solution using .Net 7. It is explained how to, using Visual Studio 2022 preview, it is easy to create a Razor Web Page and edit the information on each page.

Also, we have seen how to navigate between the pages and how to add new pages. We have also been able to learn how to integrate a simple minimal API, which will change the way our page appears.

We were able to learn and view some of the changes implemented in this version of .Net, like the fact that it doesn't contain a Startup file, like it had in previous .Net 6 version.

To finalize the chapter we have seen how it is possible to implement this application, how to make general configurations using `appsettings.json`, and had a small glimpse on the model view controller model, that we will come back later on.

Now, take a deep breath, relax, and prepare for what is coming.

In the following chapter we will go through the first part of the Model View Controller: The Views, and how to create one view from scratch, with several different elements.

Hope you enjoy the next stoppage point!

Join our book's Discord space

Join the book's Discord Workspace for Latest updates, Offers, Tech happenings around the world, New Release and Sessions with the Authors:

https://discord.bpbonline.com

CHAPTER 4
Designing the Views

Introduction

After an introduction to **.Net 7**, some history on .Net, getting to know the features and libraries of .Net 7 and comparing them to the previous version, and, learning to write our simple first program, let us now embark on the next steps of our journey.

In this chapter we will cover the View design, which was touched a bit in *Chapter 3*, but now we will detail a bit more, and show some examples of Razor views (`.cshtml` pages) and some partial views, that are very useful to be used when we need to show the same (or similar) information on different pages.

So, let us now start, open Visual Studio and let us go!

Structure

The topics that will be covered in this chapter will be:

- Create the Views
- Show some examples of possible views (in Razor) and some partials

Objectives

The goal on this chapter will be to learn and discovery how the Views work in .Net 7.

We will see how they are designed and go through two ways of View and Partial View designing and creating: using **Model View Controller** (**MVC**) and Razor Pages.

Creating the Views

The View is the visual part that the user sees, it can also be called of frontend, or user interface.

For ASP.Net **Model View Controller (MVC)** it was introduced Razor Views (`.cshtml` files) that, elegantly, help you create the HTML output with C# (hence the .cs – meaning C-Sharp or C#).

But, if you are not using MVC, you can use something similar, called Razor Pages project (like the one we have created on the previous chapter).

We will now explain how to create the views (both in MVC and Razor pages).

MVC

Starting with MVC, and after creating the MVC Project, we need to follow these steps:

1. Open the **Solution Explorer** and right-click on the **Views** folder. Then select the option **Add | View**, like it is shown in the figure:

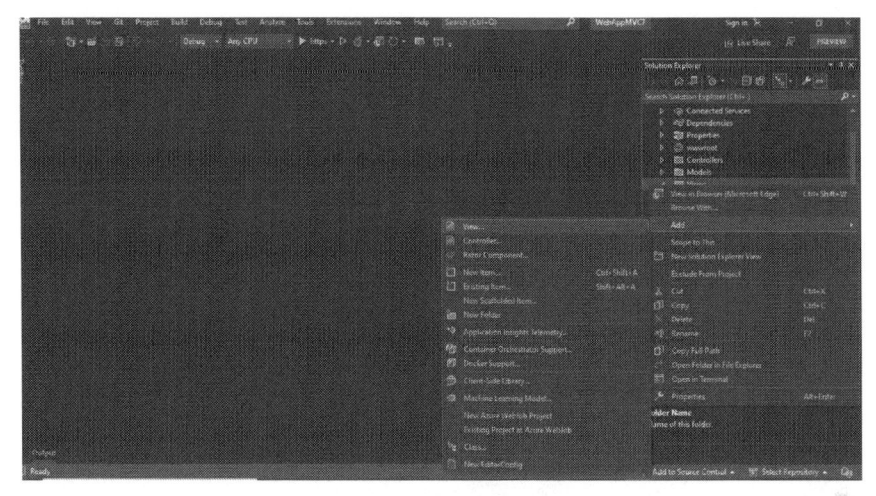

Figure 4.1: Add a View to MVC

2. Select **Razor View -Empty** and click on **Add**, like we can see in the *Figure 4.2*:

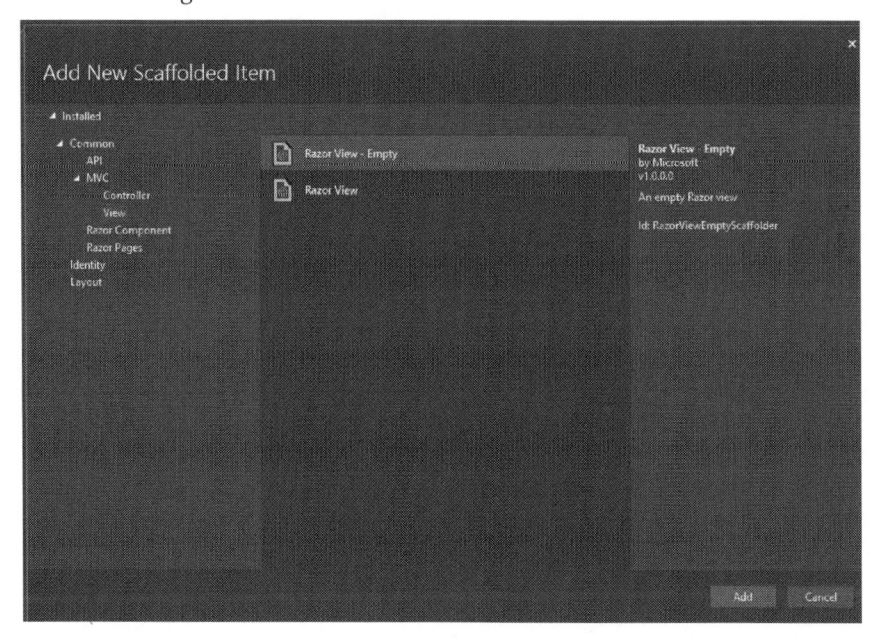

Figure 4.2: Add Razor View – Empty

3. Rename it and, again, click on **Add**, as it is shown in *Figure 4.3*:

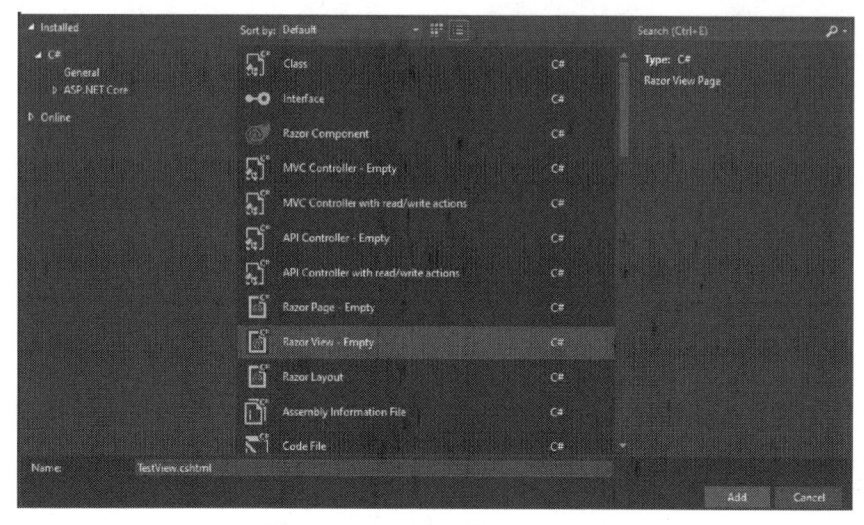

Figure 4.3: *Rename and add the view*

4. The view is now created, as it can be seen in *Figure 4.4*.! Now let us add some content.

Figure 4.4: *Created View*

1. @{
2.   ViewData["Title"] = "Test Page MVC";
3. }
4.
5. <h2>Test Page MVC</h2>
6.
7. <p>Welcome to the MVC View .Net 7!</p>

We can see how it will look, when running the application and navigating to **TestView**, as shown in *Figure 4.5*.

Figure 4.5: *TestView*

Designing the Views ■ 49

5. To run the application and create the navigation we will need to use the controllers, which will be seen in more detail in the next chapter, but just to understand and to execute this example, in the following figure, is shown, highlighted, the code that must be added in the **_Layout.cshtml** file:

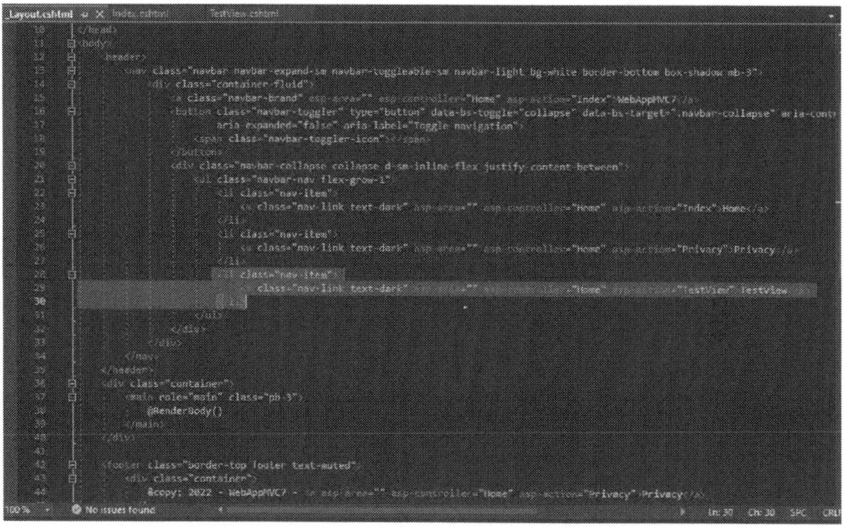

Figure 4.6: Highlighted code to add in _Layout.cshtml

6. Also, in the **HomeController.cs** it must be added a new method, as seen, highlighted, in the *Figure 4.7*:

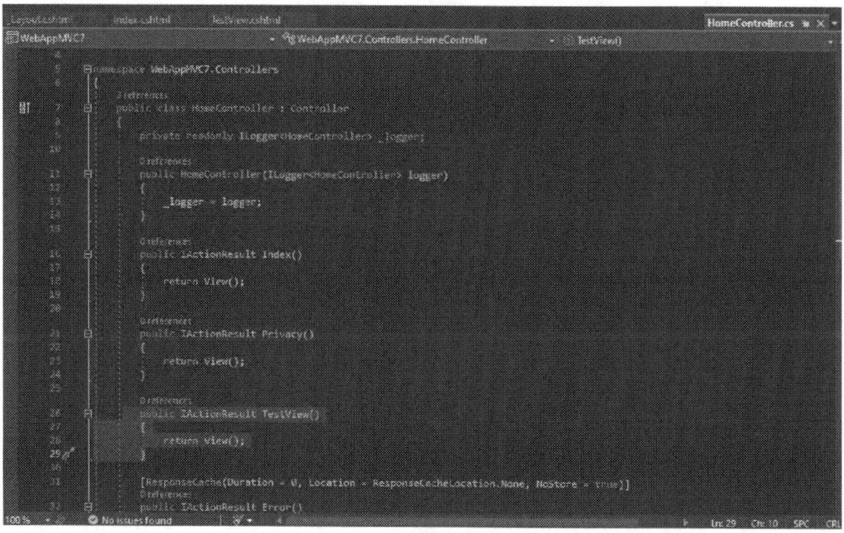

Figure 4.7: Highlighted method to add in HomeController.cs

Razor pages

Now, let us head to Razor Pages. After creating a Razor Web App Project (like we did on the example in *Chapter 3, Writing your first .Net 7 program*), we need to follow these steps:

1. Open the Solution Explorer and right-click on the **Pages** folder. Then select the option **Add | Razor Page**, like it is shown in *Figure 4.8*:

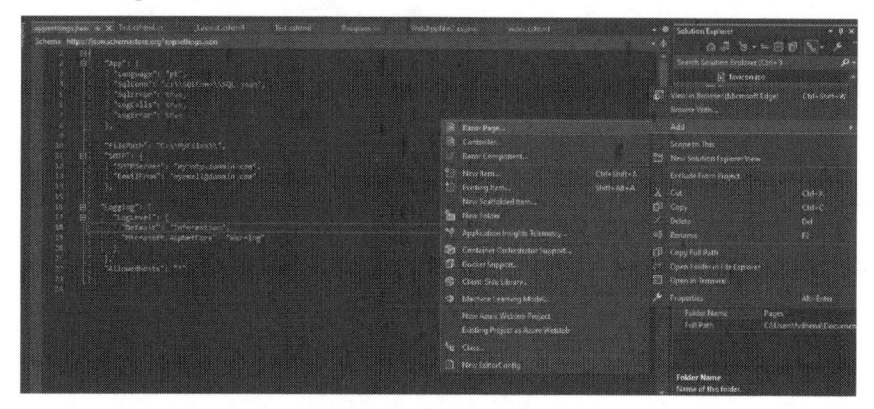

Figure 4.8: Add a Razor Page to the project

2. Select **Razor Page -Empty** and click on **Add**, like we can see in the following figure:

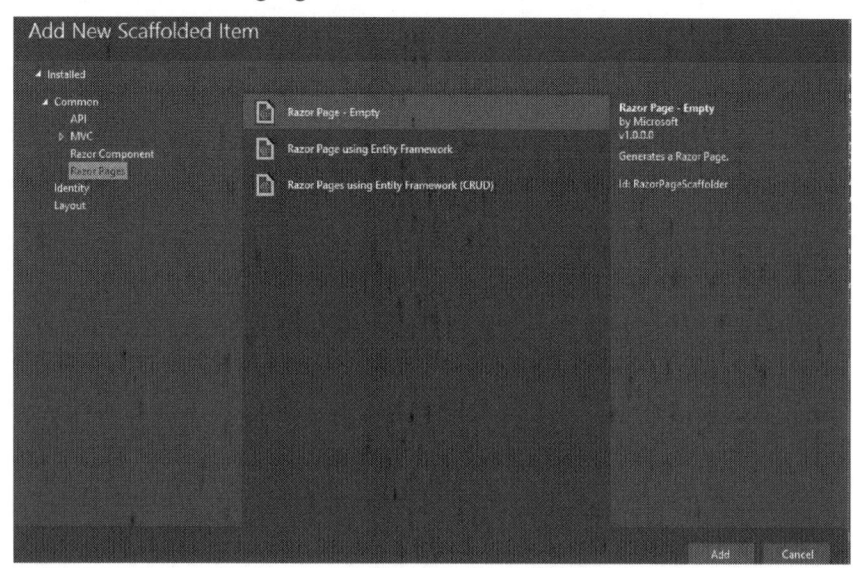

Figure 4.9: Add Razor Page – Empty

Designing the Views ■ 51

3. Rename it and, again, click on **Add**, as it is shown in *Figure 4.10*:

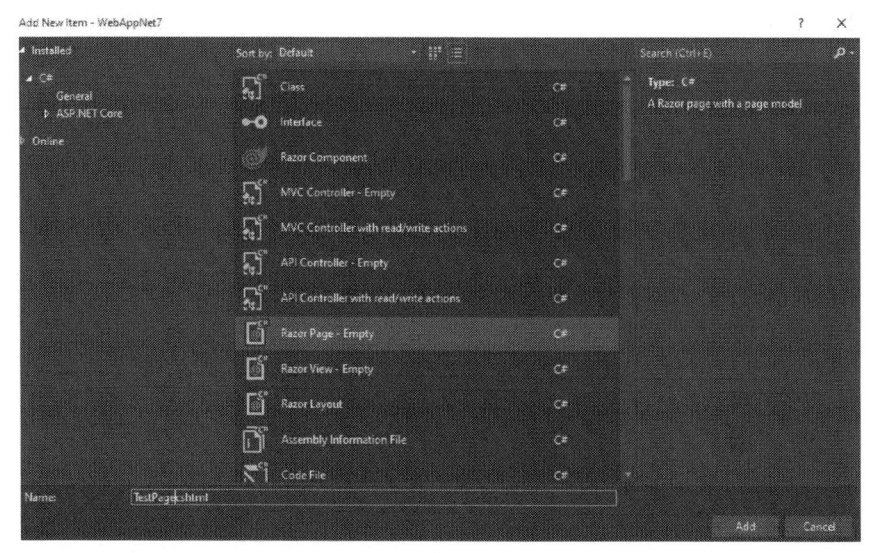

Figure 4.10: Rename and add the page

The razor page is now created! Now let us add some content.

```
1.  @page
2.  @model WebAppNet7.Pages.TestPageModel
3.  @{
4.      ViewData["Title"] = "Test Razor Page";
5.  }
6.
7.  <h2>Test Razor Page </h2>
8.
9.  <p> Welcome to the Razor Page .Net 7!</p>
```

The code is like the one created for the MVC View but it has some new concepts.

For example, it has the **@page** directive that will turn this file into an MVC action, meaning that it will be able to handle requests directly, without the need of a Controller.

We can see how it will look, when running the application and navigating to Test, as shown in *Figure 4.11*:

Figure 4.11: Test Razor Page

To run the application and create the navigation we will need to add the link to the **_Layout.cshtml** file, like it is seen, highlighted in the following figure:

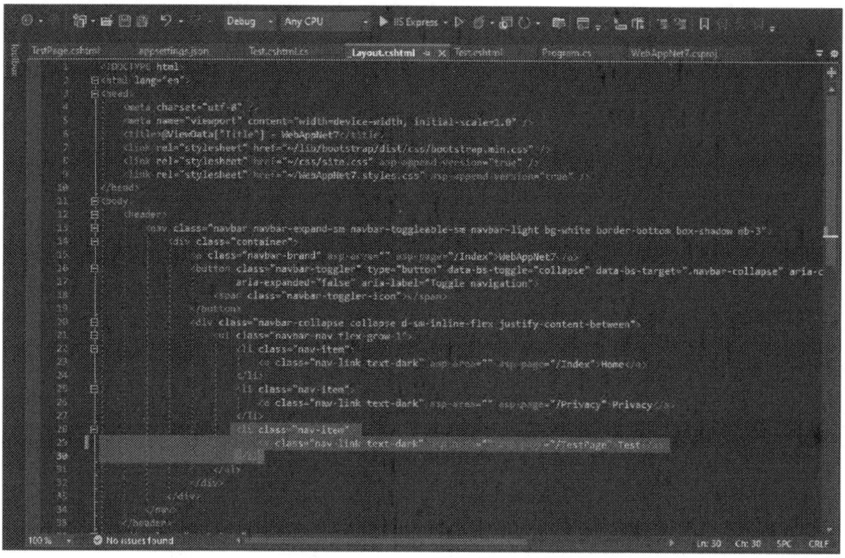

Figure 4.12: Highlighted code to add in _Layout.cshtml

Creating a partial view

Besides the views, and to complement and simplify them, we can use partial views, which are reusable portions of a web page. We can also create these partials, with or without the **PageModel** class, but usually they are created without them.

Also, one usual rule is to keep the Partials in the **Shared** folder, as they are to be used in different Pages/Views.

Like we have seen in the views, we will share some examples on how to create partial in MVC and Razor Pages.

MVC

So, lets once again start with MVC. Open your MVC project and follow these steps:

1. Open the Solution Explorer and right-click on the **Shared** subfolder inside the **Views** folder. Then select the option **Add | View**, like it is shown in *Figure 4.13*:

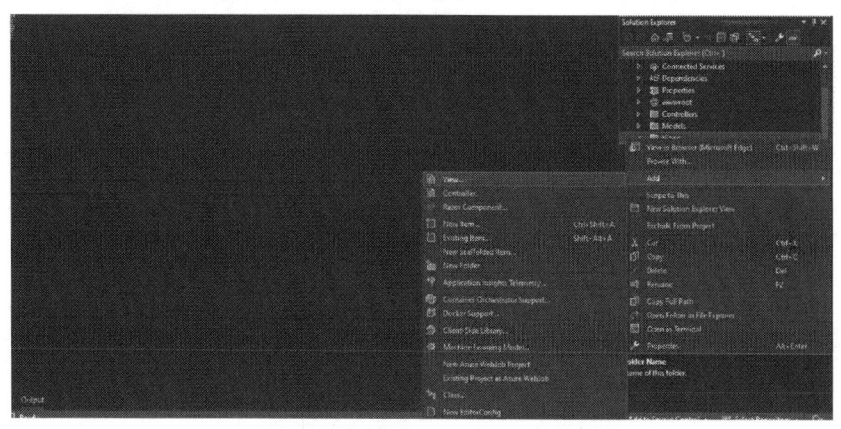

Figure 4.13: Add a Partial View to MVC

2. Select **Razor View -Empty** and click on **Add**, like we can see in the following figure:

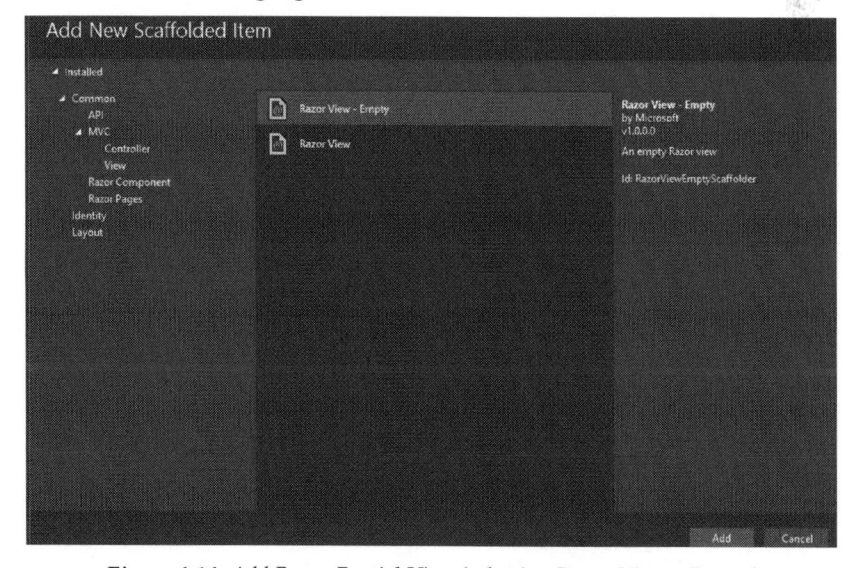

Figure 4.14: Add Razor Partial View (selecting Razor View – Empty)

54 ■ .NET 7 for Jobseekers

3. Rename it and, again, click on **Add**, as it is shown in *Figure 4.15* (usually the partials have their name starting with an underscore - '_'):

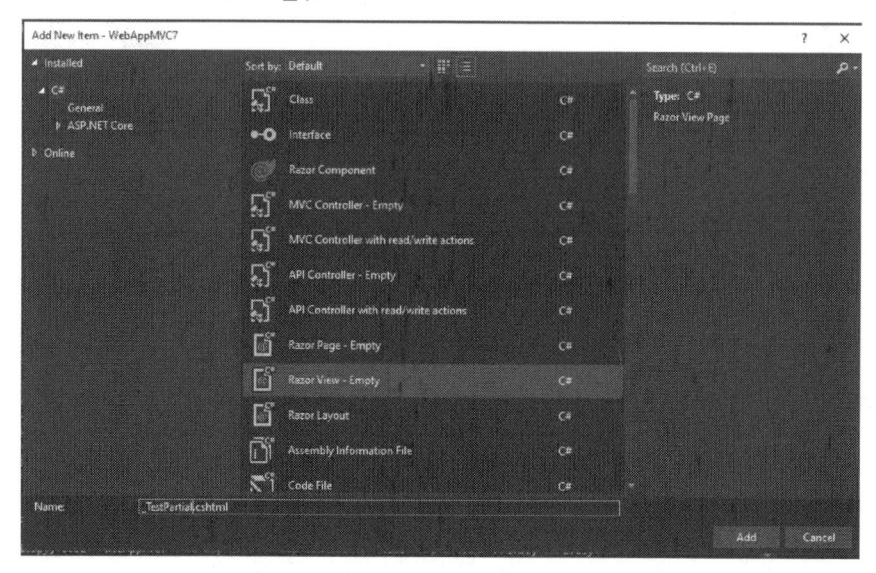

Figure 4.15: Rename and add the Partial view

4. The Partial View is now created! Now let us add some content. For example, let's get some code from the `_Layout.cshtml`, for the menu options:

```
1. <div class="navbar-collapse collapse d-sm-
   inline-flex justify-content-between">
2.     <ul class="navbar-nav flex-grow-1">
3.         <li class="nav-item">
4.             <a class="nav-link text-dark"
   asp-area="" aspcontroller="Home" asp-
   action="Index">Home</a>
5.         </li>
6.         <li class="nav-item">
7.             <a class="nav-link text-dark"
   asp-area="" aspcontroller="Home" asp-
   action="Privacy">Privacy</a>
8.         </li>
9.         <li class="nav-item">
```

```
10.            <a class="nav-link text-dark"
   asp-area="" aspcontroller="Home" asp-
   action="TestView">TestView</a>
11.         </li>
12.      </ul>
13.   </div>
```

To render the partial view in the parent View, we can use **@html. PartialAsync()** or **@html.RenderPartialAsync()**.

Let us see an example of usage of the first render option (**PartialAsync**), in the code below (line 10, in bold):

```
1. <body>
2.    <header>
3.       <nav class="navbar navbar-expand-sm navbar-
   toggleable-sm navbarlight bg-white border-bottom
   box-shadow mb-3">
4.          <div class="container-fluid">
5.             <a class="navbar-brand" asp-area=""
   aspcontroller="Home" asp-action="Index">WebAppMVC7</
   a>
6.             <button class="navbar-toggler"
   type="button" data-bstoggle="collapse" data-bs-
   target=".navbar-collapse" aria-
   controls="navbarSupportedContent"
7.                       aria-expanded="false"
   arialabel="Toggle navigation">
8.                <span class="navbar-toggler-
   icon"></span>
9.             </button>
10.            @Html.PartialAsync("_TestPartial")
11.          </div>
12.       </nav>
13.    </header>
14.    <div class="container">
15.       <main role="main" class="pb-3">
16.          @RenderBody()
```

17.   </main>
18.   </div>
19.
20.   <footer class="border-top footer text-muted">
21.   <div class="container">
22.   © 2022 - WebAppMVC7 - <a asp-area="" aspcontroller="Home" asp-action="Privacy">Privacy</a>
23.   </div>
24.   </footer>
25.   <script src="~/lib/jquery/dist/jquery.min.js"></script>
26.   <script src="~/lib/bootstrap/dist/js/bootstrap.bundle.min.js"></scri pt>
27.   <script src="~/js/site.js" asp-append-version="true"></script>
28.   @await RenderSectionAsync("Scripts", required: false)
29. </body>

Now, testing the second render (**RenderPartialAsync**), in the code below (line 9, in bold):

1. <body>
2.   <header>
3.   <nav class="navbar navbar-expand-sm navbar-toggleable-sm navbarlight bg-white border-bottom box-shadow mb-3">
4.   <div class="container-fluid">
5.   <a class="navbar-brand" asp-area="" aspcontroller="Home" asp-action="Index">WebAppMVC7</a>
6.   <button class="navbar-toggler" type="button" data-bstoggle="collapse" data-bs-target=".navbar-collapse" ariacontrols="navbarSupportedContent" aria-expanded="false" arialabel="Toggle navigation">

7.   <span class="navbar-toggler-icon"></span>
8.   </button>
9.   @Html.RenderPartialAsync("_TestPartial")
10.   </div>
11.   </nav>
12.   </header>
13.   <div class="container">
14.   <main role="main" class="pb-3">
15.   @RenderBody()
16.   </main>
17.   </div>
18.
19.   <footer class="border-top footer text-muted">
20.   <div class="container">
21.   © 2022 - WebAppMVC7 - <a asp-area="" aspcontroller="Home" asp-action="Privacy">Privacy</a>
22.   </div>
23.   </footer>
24.   <script src="~/lib/jquery/dist/jquery.min.js"></script>
25.   <script src="~/lib/bootstrap/dist/js/bootstrap.bundle.min.js"></scri pt>
26.   <script src="~/js/site.js" asp-append-version="true"></script>
27.   @await RenderSectionAsync("Scripts", required: false)
28. </body>

Executing our MVC application, for each render type, will return the page as shown in *Figure 4.16*:

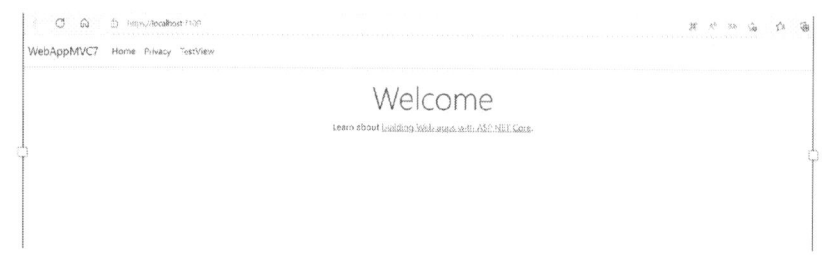

Figure 4.16: MVC application with Menu rendered from a Partial View

Razor pages

Now, getting back to Razor Pages, lets open our Razor Pages project and follow these steps:

1. Open the **Solution Explorer** and right-click on the **Pages** folder. Then select the option **Add | Razor Page,** like it is shown in *Figure 4.17:*

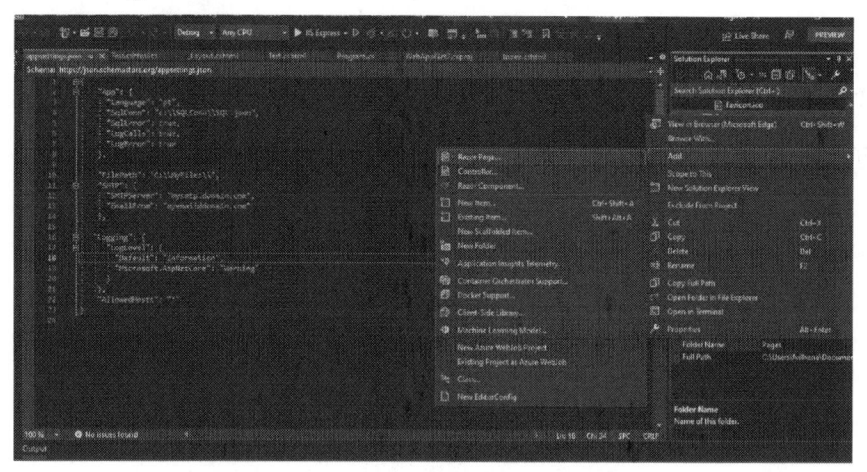

Figure 4.17: Add a Razor Partial Page to the project

2. Select **Razor Page -Empty** and click on **Add**, like we can see in the following figure:

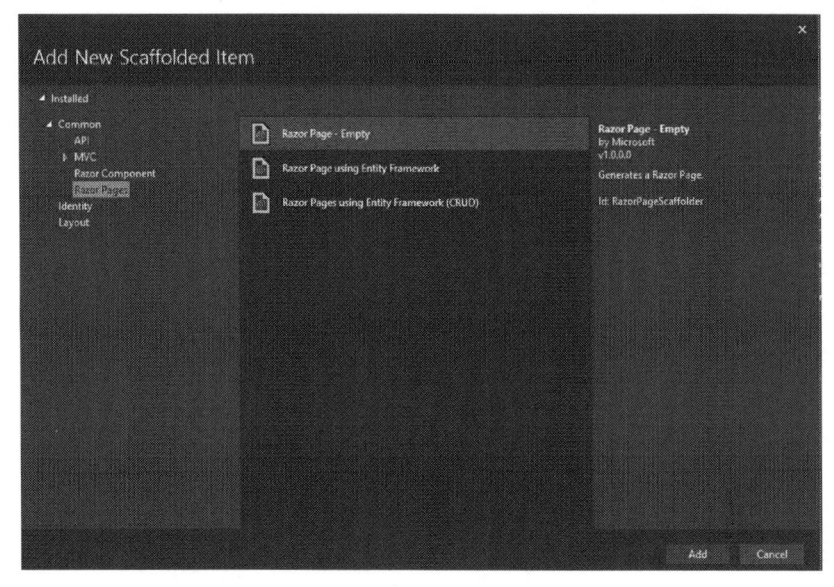

Figure 4.18: Select Razor Page – Empty to create the Partial

3. Rename it and, again, click on **Add**, as it is shown in *Figure 4.19*:

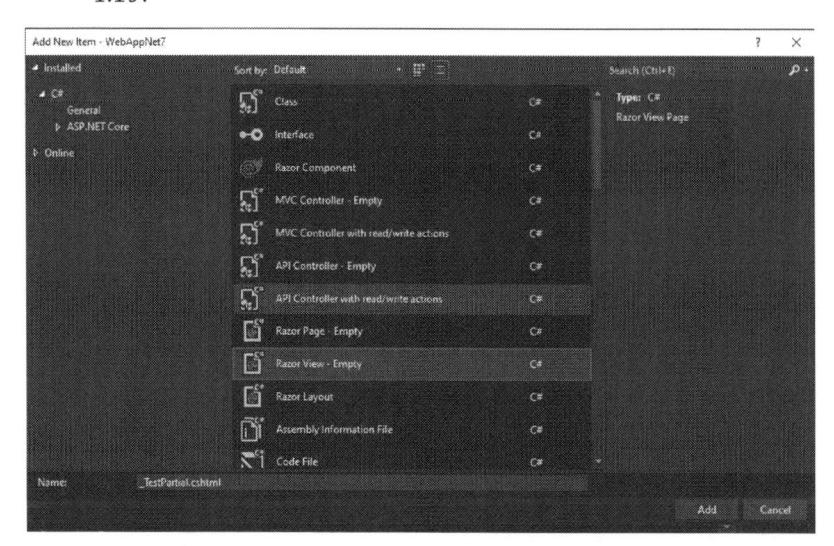

Figure 4.19: Rename and add the Razor Partial View

4. The razor partial view is now created! Now let us add some content. Like in the MVC example, lets add the menu part of the **_Layout.cshtml**:

1. <div class="navbar-collapse collapse d-sm-inline-flex justify-content- between">
2.   <ul class="navbar-nav flex-grow-1">
3.   <li class="nav-item">
4.   <a class="nav-link text-dark" asp-area="" aspcontroller="Home" asp-action="Index">Home</a>
5.   </li>
6.   <li class="nav-item">
7.   <a class="nav-link text-dark" asp-area="" aspcontroller="Home" asp-action="Privacy">Privacy</a>
8.   </li>
9.   <li class="nav-item">
10.   <a class="nav-link text-dark" asp-area="" asp-   controller="Home" asp-action="TestView">TestView</a>
11.   </li>
12.   </ul>
13. </div>

Now, in this case, to render the partial view to the Razor page we can use this simple Tag **@Html.Partial()**, as it is shown in the code below (line 9 in bold):

1. <header>
2.   <nav class="navbar navbar-expand-sm navbar-toggleable-sm navbarlight bg-white border-bottom box-shadow mb-3">
3.   <div class="container">
4.   <a class="navbar-brand" asp-area="" asppage="/Index">WebAppNet7</a>
5.   <button class="navbar-toggler" type="button" data-bstoggle="collapse" data-bs-target=".navbar-collapse" ariacontrols="navbarSupportedContent"
6. aria-expanded="false" arialabel="Toggle navigation">

```
 7. <span class="navbar-toggler-icon"></span>
 8. </button>
 9. @await Html.PartialAsync("~/Pages/Shared/_
    TestPartial.cshtml")
10. </div>
11. </nav>
12. </header>
```

When we execute the Razor Application, we will have a page with the menu created in a Partial View, as shown in *Figure 4.20*:

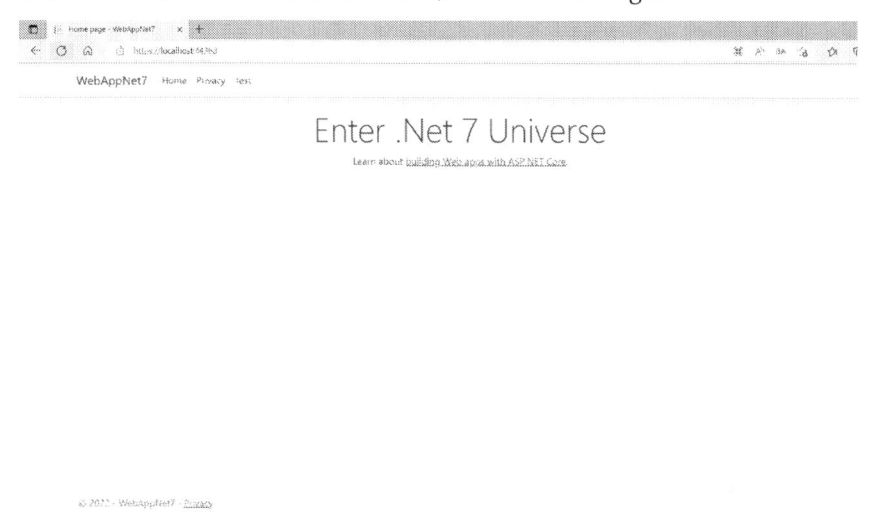

Figure 4.20: Razor Page with menu in a Partial View

Conclusion

In this chapter we have seen how to create simple views, using two different ways (MVC and Razor Pages). We were able to see the differences between these two types of usage, although it will depend on the project that you will implement.

Also, we have seen how to create Partial views and pages, and what these Partials will be used for.

Throughout all the process, besides some explanations, we have shown some examples and guides to walkthrough these steps.

So, let us now rest and prepare for the next chapter, on which we will continue this journey, travelling to the second part of the MVC: the controller.

Hope you will have a great time!

Join our book's Discord space

Join the book's Discord Workspace for Latest updates, Offers, Tech happenings around the world, New Release and Sessions with the Authors:

https://discord.bpbonline.com

CHAPTER 5
Creating Your Controllers

Introduction

Travelling in this journey we are getting to know a bit more about .Net 7 and its features. In the last chapter we have talked about **Model View Controller** (**MVC**) methodology and covered one of the parts of it: the Views.

Now, it's time to get to know the other two parts, one of them a bit better: the Controller.

We will see how to create a controller in .Net 7, show some examples of controllers and, explain how it will connect with the views and the Models.

So, let's get started! We need to open Visual Studio and we are ready for this new step in our trip.

Structure

The topics that will be covered in this chapter will be:
- Creating a simple Controller

- Integrating the Controller with the View
- Creating and use some Models

Objectives

In this chapter, the objectives are to learn how to work with controllers, by showing how to create a simple controller, and integrate it afterwards with the view. Also, we will be able to learn a bit about models and how they can be used.

Creating a simple Controller

The Controller is the backend part of an MVC application and the connector between the model and the view. It will handle any incoming URL Request and will contain public Action methods, allowing to retrieve model data and returning the responses to the view.

A Controller class is recommended to end with the word "**Controller**", in order it is easier to identify and organize. Every `controller` class is recommended to be placed inside the `Controllers` folder of the MVC solution as illustrated in *Figure 5.1*:

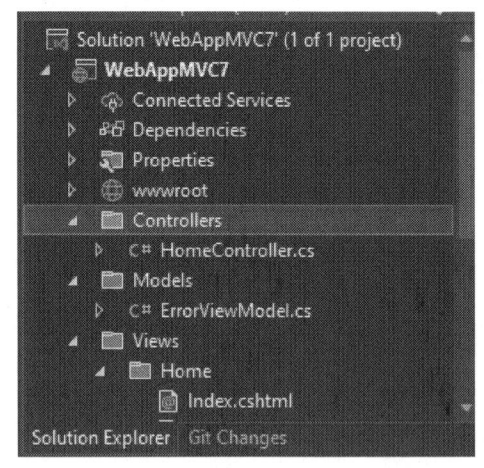

Figure 5.1: Controllers folder in the MVC Solution Explorer

So, now let us learn how to add and create a simple controller by the following steps:

Creating Your Controllers ■ 65

1. Open the **Solution Explorer** and right-click on the `Controllers` folder. Then select the option **Add** | **Controller**, like it is shown in the following figure:

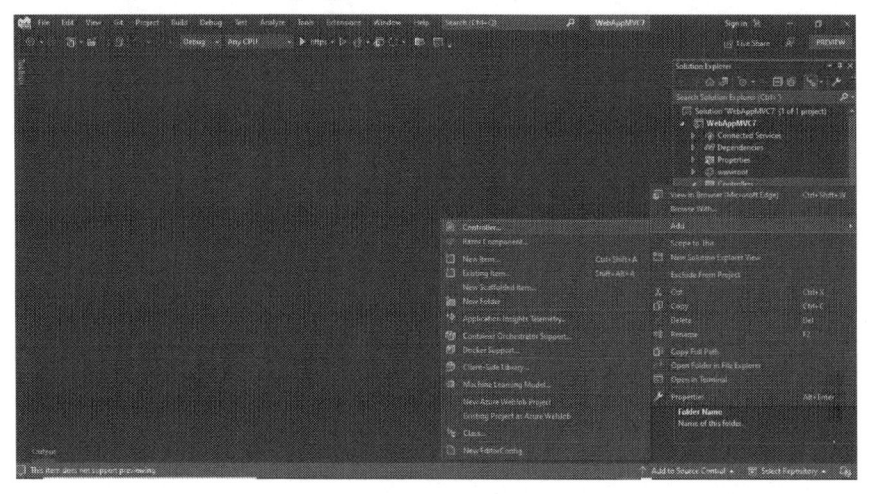

Figure 5.2: *Add a Controller to MVC*

2. Select **MVC Controller -Empty** and click on **Add**, like we can see in the following figure:

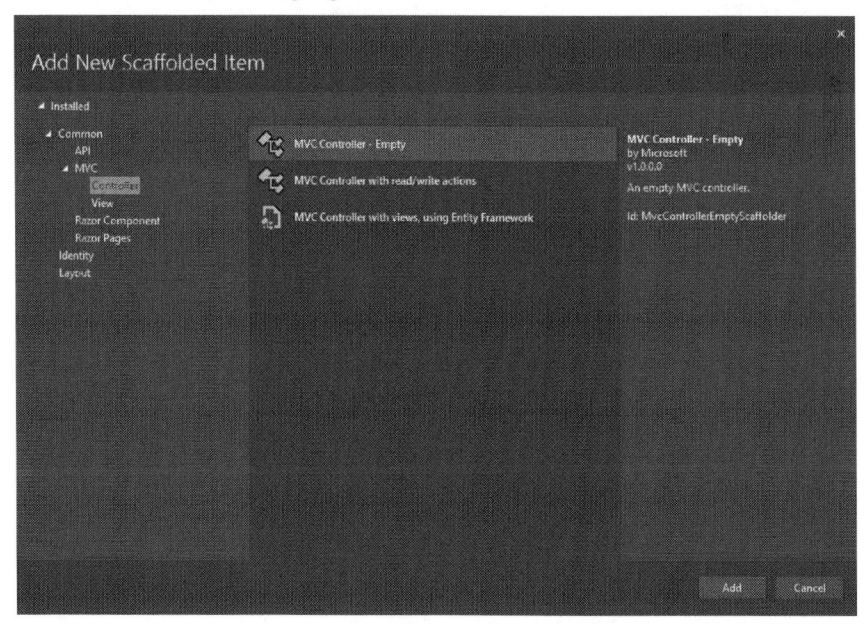

Figure 5.3: *Add MVC Controller - Empty*

66 ■ .NET 7 for Jobseekers

3. Rename it and, again, click on **Add**, as it is shown in *Figure 5.4*:

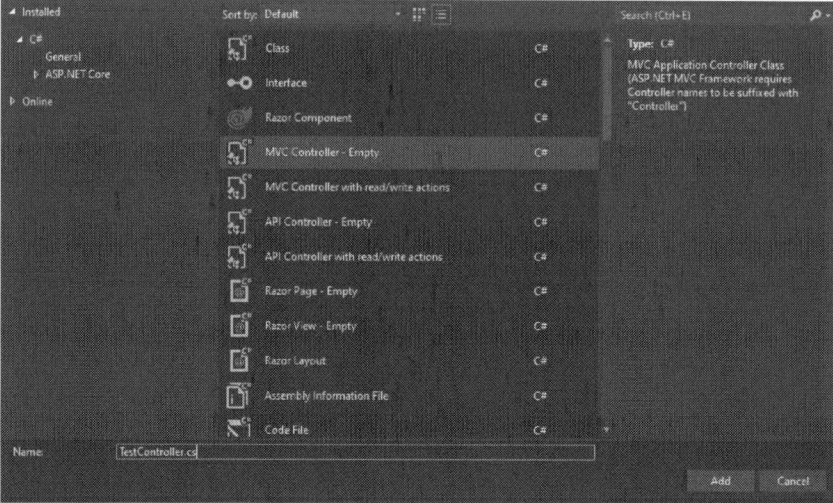

Figure 5.4: Rename and add the Controller

4. The Controller is now created! Let us see how it will stand, in the following figure:

Figure 5.5: Code base of the newly created Controller

5. Now, let us try to change a bit our controller by, for example, changing the return to a simple text string, as depicted in the following code:

```
1.  using Microsoft.AspNetCore.Mvc;
2.
3.  namespace WebAppMVC7.Controllers
4.  {
5.      public class TestController : Controller
6.      {
7.          public string Index()
8.          {
9.              return "Welcome to the Controllers in .
    Net 7!";
10.         }
11.     }
12. }
```

We can see how it will look, when running the application and navigating to **http://localhost/test_** or **http://localhost/test/index_** as shown in *Figure 5.6*:

Figure 5.6: Test Controller

Integrating the Controller with the View

Now, let us continue and integrate the controller we have created with a view.

Let us use the Partial View we've created in the previous chapter (**_TestPartial.cshtml**), pictured next:

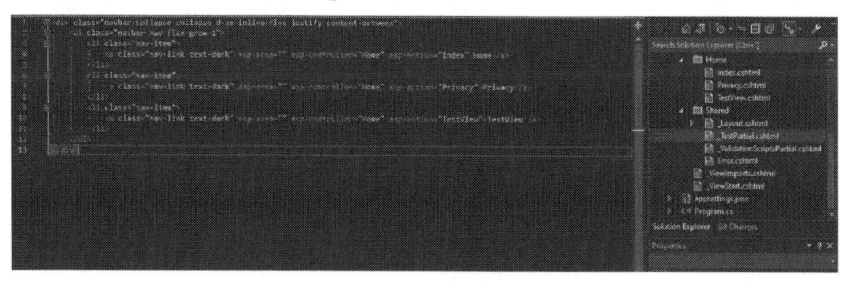

Figure 5.7: _TestPartial.cshtml partial view

As we can see, the code is pointing to our Home Controller:

```
1.          <li class="nav-item">
2.              <a class="nav-link text-dark" asp-area="" asp-controller="Home" asp-action="Index">Home</a>
3.          </li>
4.          <li class="nav-item">
5.              <a class="nav-link text-dark" asp-area="" aspcontroller="Home" asp-action="Privacy">Privacy</a>
6.          </li>
7.          <li class="nav-item">
8.              <a class="nav-link text-dark" asp-area="" aspcontroller="Home" asp-action="TestView">TestView</a>
9.          </li>
```

So, let us change this, and point the code to our newly created Test Controller, replacing it in the asp-controller.

```
1.          <li class="nav-item">
2.              <a class="nav-link text-dark" asp-area="" aspcontroller="Test" asp-action="Index">Home</a>
3.          </li>
4.          <li class="nav-item">
5.              <a class="nav-link text-dark" asp-area="" aspcontroller="Test" asp-action="Privacy">Privacy</a>
6.          </li>
7.          <li class="nav-item">
8.              <a class="nav-link text-dark" asp-area="" aspcontroller="Test" asp-action="TestView">TestView</a>
9.          </li>
```

But this is not enough, because, if we try to run the application and open the links on the menu, we will have the error pictured in the following figure:

Hmmm... can't reach this page localhost

No page was found to the web address:

https://localhost:7109/Test/TestView

HTTP ERROR 404

Update

Figure 5.8: Error navigating to the menu

So, to avoid the error, we must configure the connection between the view and the controller.

Let us then open **TestController.cs**. We need to add the methods for each of the actions we will do:

```
1.    public IActionResult Index()
2.    {
3.        return View();
4.    }
5.
6.    public IActionResult Privacy()
7.    {
8.        return View();
9.    }
10.
11.   public string TestView()
12.   {
13.       return "Welcome to the Controllers in .Net 7!";
14.   }
```

We will have, for now, the **TestView** method returning our test phrase, instead of the view, as the others do.

We will also need to change the name of the folder where the views are placed. Now we have the following:

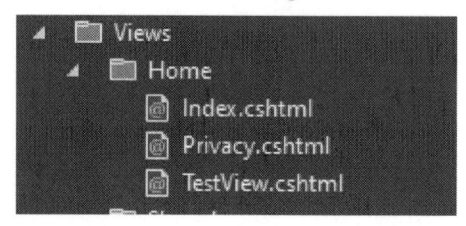

Figure 5.9: Current Views folder in Solution Explorer

We will have to change the folder from **"Home"** to **"Test"**, as depicted in the following figure:

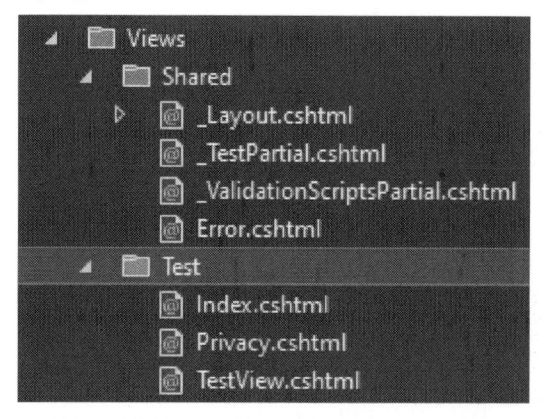

Figure 5.10: Changed folder name in the Views folder, in Solution Explorer

Now, running the app we will get the following, as shown in *Figure 5.11*:

Figure 5.11: Index View using TestController.cshtml

And, if we navigate to TestView, we will have our string, as shown in *Figure 5.12*:

Figure 5.12: *TestView using TestController.cshtml*

Let us now change the code of `TestView` method in the `TestController`:

```
1.    public string TestView()
2.    {
3.        return View();
4.    }
```

Run the application again and check what happens when navigating to the view as depicted in *Figure 5.13*:

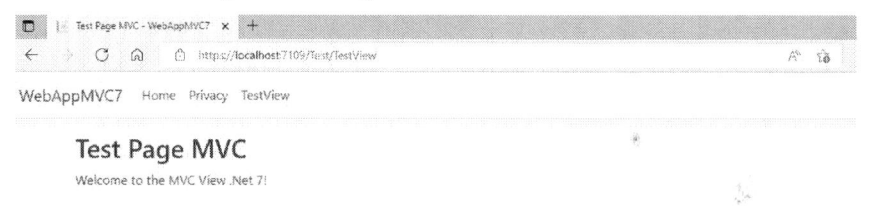

Figure 5.13: *Navigation to TestView using TestController.cshtml and IActionResult method*

Creating and using a Model

The Model classes are the last part of an **Model View Controller (MVC)** app, and represent the connection to database, object construction and more, which will then be connected to the *Views*.

72 ■ .NET 7 for Jobseekers

Adding a Model Class

Go to the **Solution Explorer** and, right-click on the **Models** folder, then select **Add | Class**, as shown in the following figure:

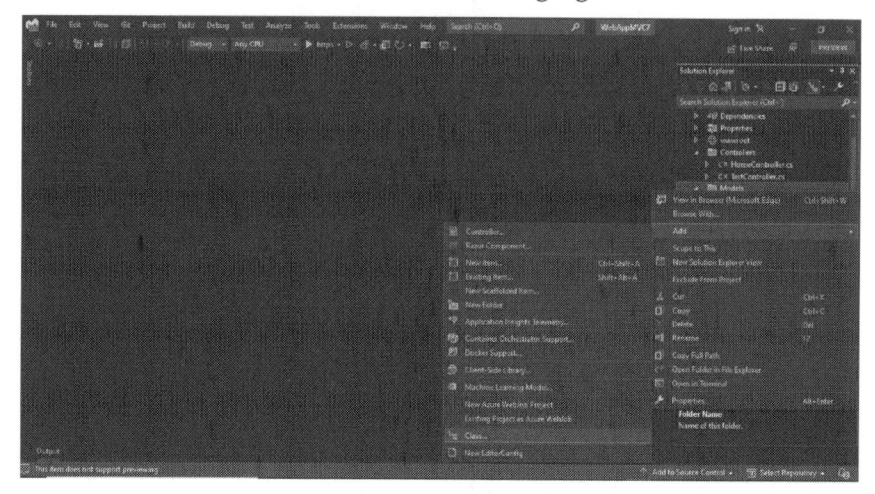

Figure 5.14: Add new Model Class

Rename it and click on **Add**, as it is shown in *Figure 5.15*:

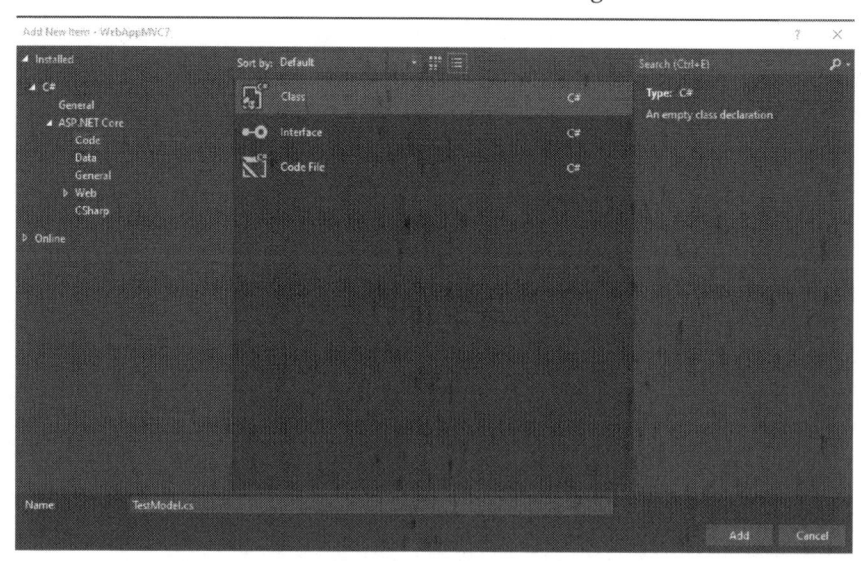

Figure 5.15: Rename and add the class

Creating Your Controllers ■ 73

It will generate a class like it is shown in *Figure 5.16*:

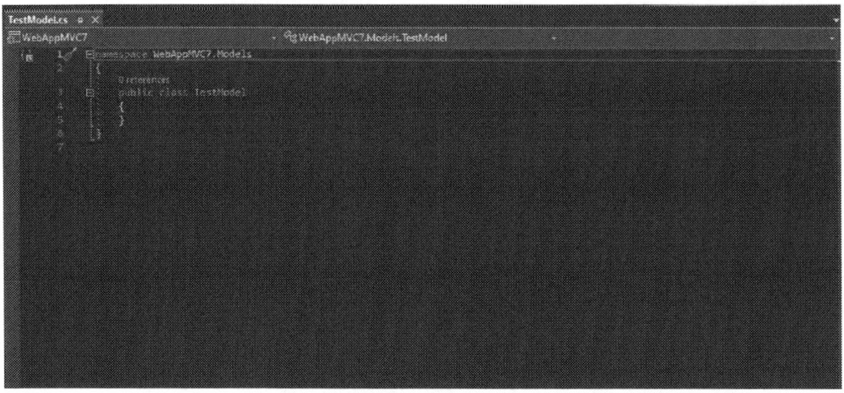

Figure 5.16: Model Class

Now let us add some code to the Model class. We will add some properties to be shown on our view:

```
1.  using System.ComponentModel.DataAnnotations;
2.
3.  namespace WebAppMVC7.Models
4.  {
5.      public class TestModel
6.      {
7.          public int Id { get; set; }
8.          public string? Name { get; set; }
9.
10.         [DataType(DataType.Date)]
11.         public DateTime? RegisterDate { get; set; } = new DateTime();
12.         public string? Testfield { get; set; }
13.     }
14. }
```

After this let us use the scaffolding tool to produce CRUD pages for the model (Create, Read, Update and Delete).

74 ■ .NET 7 for Jobseekers

To do so, in solution explorer, right-click on **Controller** folder and
Add | New Scaffolded Item, as shown in the following figure:

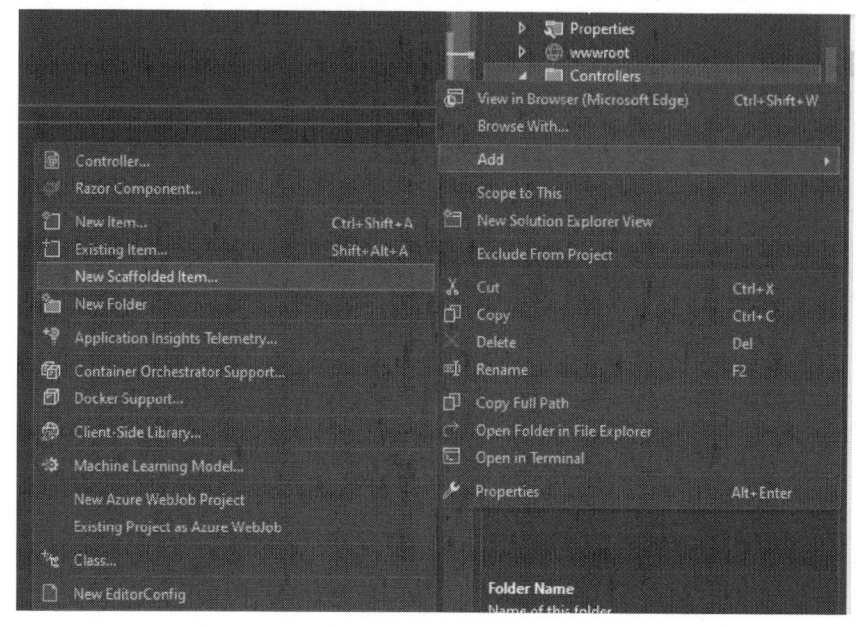

Figure 5.17: Add Scaffolded Item

In the following screen, select "**MVC Controller With views, using Entity Framework**" and click **Add**, as shown in *Figure 5.18*:

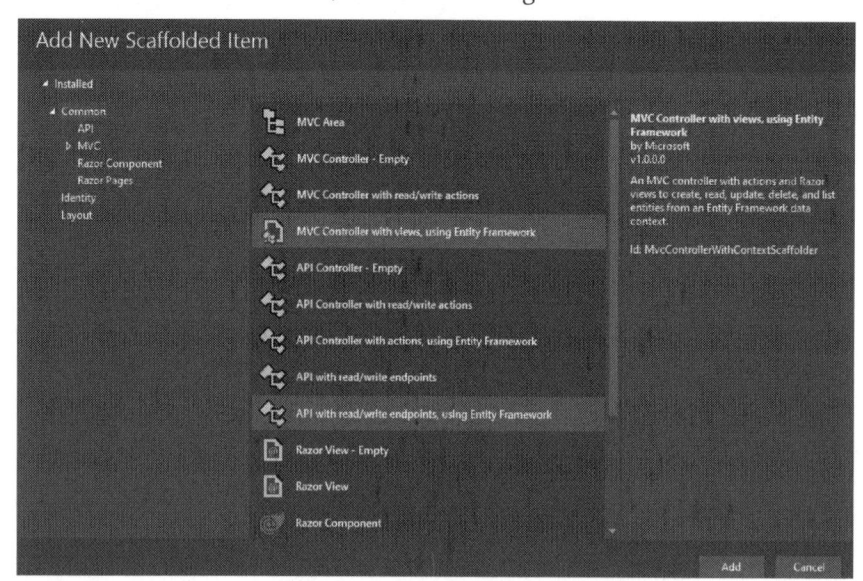

Figure 5.18: Select Scaffolding option

Creating Your Controllers ■ 75

On the next step, select the **Model Class** you want, then, on the **Data Context Class**, click on the **Plus sign (+)** and then Add the result. Leave the rest as is, and then click **add**. You can see how it will look, in the following figure:

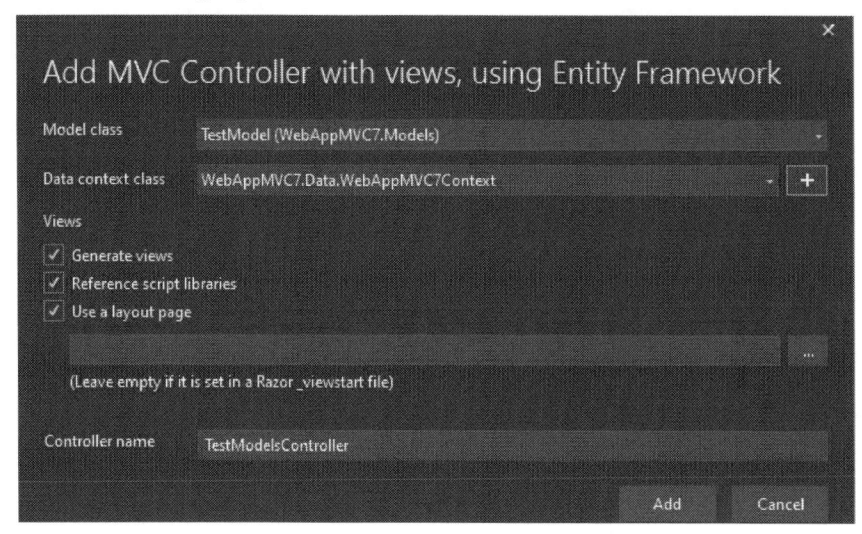

Figure 5.19: Fill Scaffolding options

The Scaffolding may take a while to run as it will add Nuget Packages and insert the required references in our project file, it will also set the database connection string and store in the **appsettings.json** file and register the database context on **Program.cs**.

Once it is done you will have a Controller created in the **Controllers** folder, view files for **Create**, **Delete**, **Details**, **Edit** and **Index** pages in **Views/TestModel** folder, and a database context class in **Data** folder. You can see how it will be in the Solution Explorer, in *Figure 5.20*:

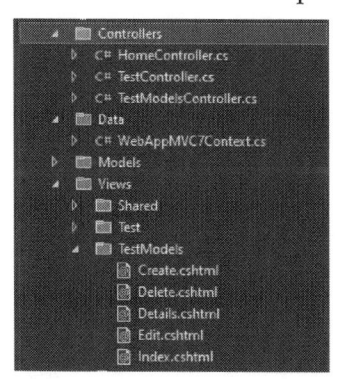

Figure 5.20: Scaffolded created files, shown in the Solution Explorer

If we try to execute our solution and navigate to the Views created with scaffolding, we will get an error because there is no database created yet. Ahead, we will learn how to integrate this with the database and then we will be able to test these Views.

Conclusion

In this chapter we have seen how to create the controllers and how to integrate it with the views, using our previous MVC project.

We were able to learn how to create a Model and with it, create some views and a controller, using Scaffolding.

Throughout all the process, besides some explanations, we have shown some examples and guides to walkthrough the steps.

With this we have seen all the three parts of the MVC methodology: The Views, in chapter 4, and now, the Controller and Models.

So, let us now sit back, take a deep breath, and get ready for the next chapter, where we will learn how to test our Views and Controller.

Hope you are enjoying and will have a great time!

Join our book's Discord space

Join the book's Discord Workspace for Latest updates, Offers, Tech happenings around the world, New Release and Sessions with the Authors:

https://discord.bpbonline.com

CHAPTER 6
Testing Your Views and Controllers

Introduction

We are learning a lot and having lots of fun in our journey through .Net 7!

After learning about all the MVC components, finishing up in last chapter, with the Controller – and a bit of the Models – we will now learn how to Test everything, by creating unit tests.

Usually, after finishing the development, we perform our tests and check if everything is OK.

But, to verify the code, we can create unit tests, which is a method by which individual units of the source code are tested automatically, to determine if they are fit for use.

So, let us then begin and start this part of our journey and learn more about unit tests and it is applicability and usage in .Net 7.

Structure

The topics that will be covered in this chapter will be:

- Unit tests

- How to perform tests and debug

Objectives

This chapter has the objective to show how to create and use Unit Tests and also help you learn how to perform simple testing and debugging.

Unit tests

To do more automatic and controlled tests – besides the typical debug, using F5 – we can set up unit testing.

So, first, we will show how to create unit tests for Controllers by using the following steps:

1. Add a new Controller, like it was seen in the previous chapters. Our Controller will be renamed as **UnitTestController.cs** and will have the menu methods, to retrieve each view, like it can be seen in the *Figure 6.1*:

   ```
   using Microsoft.AspNetCore.Mvc;

   namespace WebAppMVC7.Controllers
   {
       public class UnitTestController : Controller
       {
           public IActionResult Index()
           {
               return View();
           }

           public IActionResult Privacy()
           {
               return View();
           }

           public IActionResult TestView()
           {
               return View();
           }
       }
   }
   ```

   Figure 6.1: Unit Test Controller

2. To test, for example, if the right view is being called, we will create a new class to perform the tests. For this example, it will be stored inside the Controllers folder and will check if each method in the **UnitTestController** will return the right view. We can see the code in *Figure 6.2*:

Figure 6.2: Testing Controller

The code above will contain three major points:

- The creation of a new instance of **UnitTestController**, in the first line.

- The invoking of the method we want to test (which is repeated for each method).

- Checking whether the view is the correct one or not (also this action is repeated for each View).

So, to run this unit test, you can press the keys *Ctrl+R,A.* or choose the option in the menu, as it can be seen in *Figure 6.3*. It will open the **Test Explorer**, where you will be able to see the test results:

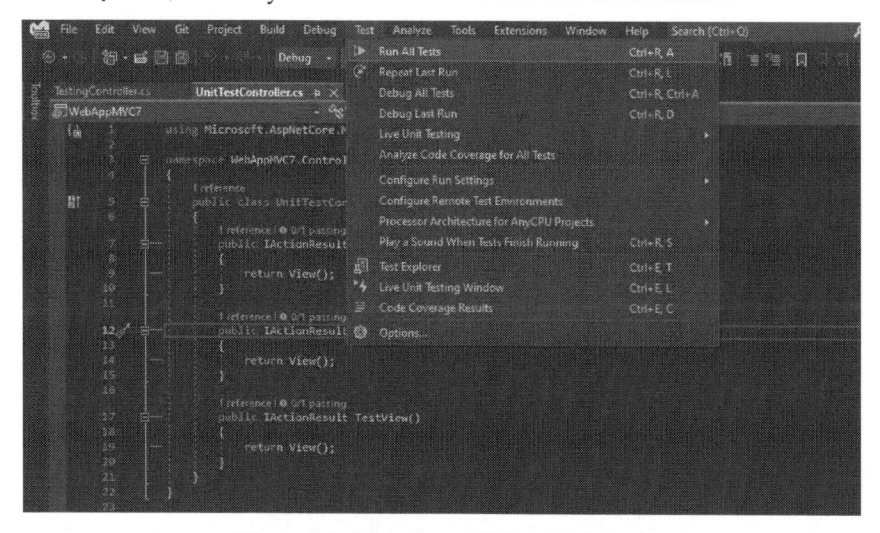

Figure 6.3: Select Run All Tests (Ctrl+R,A)

When you execute the test, it will show the Test Explorer, showing the results of the executed tests. We can see an example of the Test Explorer in the following figure:

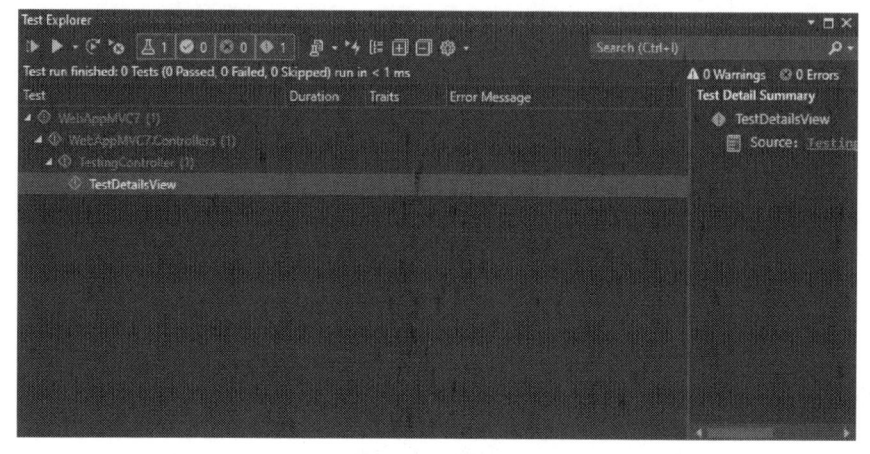

Figure 6.4: Test Explorer

Performing tests and debug

Besides the way seen in the previous point, using Unit Tests, we can test and debug our programs, in a simpler way. This can be used if we don't need Unit Tests or even, having them, we can always test and debug as it will be now described.

Just by pressing F5 or selecting the menu option **Debug | Start Debugging** you can execute your application and, placing breakpoints, analyze the code and find out the errors you may have in the code (*Figure 6.5*):

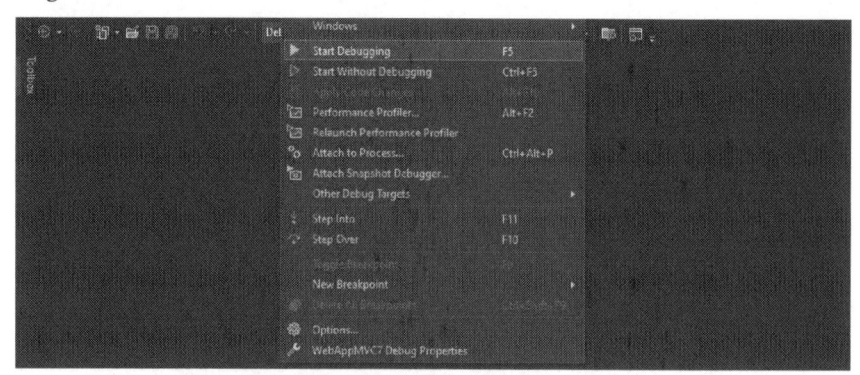

Figure 6.5: Start Debugging your application

We can set the breakpoints we need and, after running the application, and pressing the *F5*, it will stop on them. For example, if we set breakpoints in every menu call, when we select one option, it will stop on the action, like shown below:

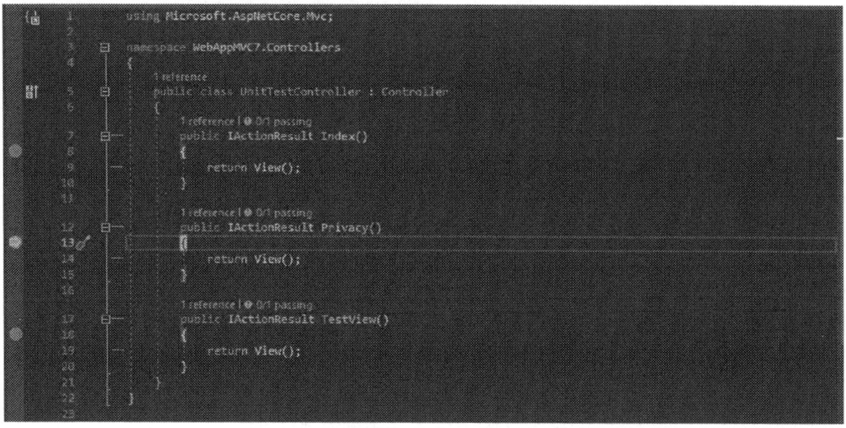

Figure 6.6: Breakpoints

If everything is OK, the page will be shown. If not, it will show the error, but it will help in order to identify and correct it.

Advantages of unit tests

Unit tests can have a lot of advantages to be used, although they can be more complex to set up as seen before in this chapter.

Let us see some advantages of unit testing:

- With it, it will be easier and safer to refactor the code, by using tests to make sure it will be done without problems and disruption. It takes the risk out of changing older source code.
- It will be kind of a quality assurance, as the Unit Tests will show problems and bugs before the product has an integration test. Creating Unit tests before the coding is completed will help to solve issues.
- They will help find problems and resolve them before further testing, in order it won't have impact in other parts of the code.
- It will simplify the integration as it will find changes and help maintain and adjust the code, by reducing bugs and defects.

- This test type will create documentation that will help understand the unit's interface.
- Unit tests will also makes debugging easier.
- It will help you to write better code and design.
- With unit tests you can reduce the cost of your project.

Conclusion

In this chapter we have seen how to create Unit Tests, that will provide useful help in testing our Controllers and Views.

Also, we have seen the simpler way of testing and debugging. This is used by developers many times a day – all of us will use it a lot (just press *F5*, cross your fingers and hope it will run correctly.

Not always work, and then it is time to debug).

These points had some examples to illustrate how to use it. It is pretty much the same as earlier versions of .Net.

Now, it is time to relax a bit and prepare for the next chapter, where we will go through one of the most interesting news that Microsoft added to the latest versions of .Net (6 and 7), at least for me, which is .Net MAUI.

Hoping you will enjoy and learn how to work with this awesome new platform.

Join our book's Discord space

Join the book's Discord Workspace for Latest updates, Offers, Tech happenings around the world, New Release and Sessions with the Authors:

https://discord.bpbonline.com

CHAPTER 7
Working with .NET MAUI

Introduction

Well, quite a ride we are having.

Now let us enter the world of one new component: .Net MAUI. This is a new **Multi-platform Application User Interface (MAUI)**, that is a framework that works cross-platforms and create native mobile and desktop applications using C# and XAML.

This was presented in .Net 6 and is having major enhancements for .Net 7.

In this chapter we will learn a bit about this framework and how to integrate it with different platforms.

We will learn what is .Net MAUI, what are the new functionalities it has for .Net 7 and how to use it in a .Net 7 application. Also, we will see different libraries and platform specific frameworks for iOS, Android, macOS, Window. In *Figure 7.1*, taken from Microsoft DevBlogs, we can see how it will look like.

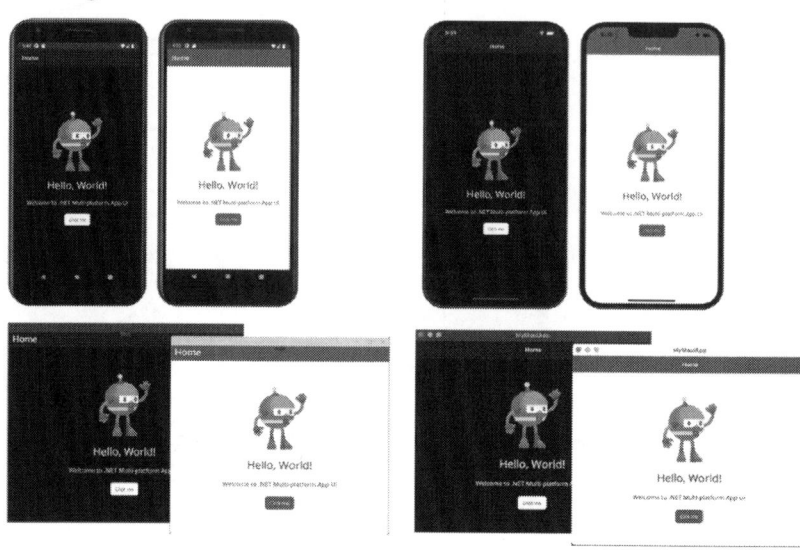

Figure 7.1: *.Net MAUI single project in different platforms*

It is now time to relax and begin this path, learning and travelling to the hidden word of .Net MAUI.

Structure

The topics that will be covered in this chapter will be:

- .Net MAUI In a nutshell
- New Functionalities in .Net MAUI
- Use .Net MAUI in a .Net 7 Application
- Different Libraries and Platform specific Frameworks: iOS, Android, macOS, Windows.

Objectives

This chapter has the objective of learning more about this new feature, presented in .Net 6, that is used as an upgrade to Xamarin: .Net MAUI.

We will see what this really is, get to know what .Net 7 brings new and how to use it in a .Net 7 application. Also, we will learn about different libraries and platform specific frameworks.

.Net MAUI in a nutshell

First, let us analyse the etymology: MAUI = Multi-platform Application User Interface.

So, now that we know what MAUI stands for, a quick explanation on what it is and what it is for: .Net MAUI is a framework, that works cross-platform, and is used to create native mobile and desktop apps using C# and XAML.

You can use it to develop apps that can run on different platforms, such as Android, iOS, macOS and Windows, using a single shared code base. It is open source and is an evolution of Xamarin (which was Microsoft open-source platform to build iOS, Android, and Windows with .Net, using an abstraction layer to manage the communication of shared code with the platform code). But, as this is an evolution, it has some improvements, regarding Xamarin. You can now create multi-platform apps using a single project but being able to add platform-specific source code and resources.

.Net MAUI focus on enabling the implementation of most of the app logic and UI layout in a single code base.

In *Figure 7.2* we can see a design from Microsoft learning page, on how MAUI was designed (for .Net 6).

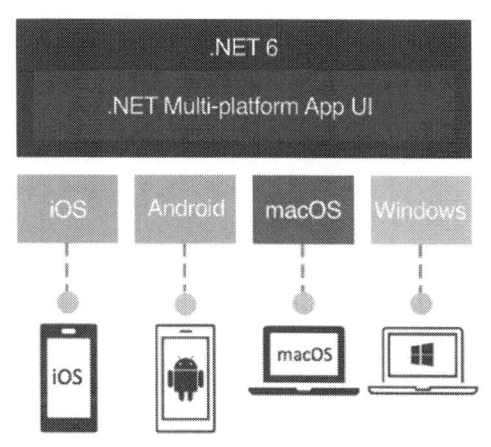

Figure 7.2: .Net MAUI design

.Net MAUI is created for developers that wish to:

- Create, in Visual Studio, cross-platform apps, using C#, from a single shared code base.

- Share UI layout and design or code, tests, and business logic, between different platforms.

But, how does .Net MAUI works?

Well, it will unify Android, iOS, macOS and Windows APIs to a single API, so that it will generate a better developing experience, by letting us write the code only once, and it will run in any of the platforms. It will also provide profound access to every aspect of each platform.

So, in general, .Net MAUI will provide a single framework for building **User Interfaces (UI)** for mobile and desktop apps. It is shown in the following diagram, from Microsoft Learning, with the high-level view of .Net MAUI app architecture (for .Net 6):

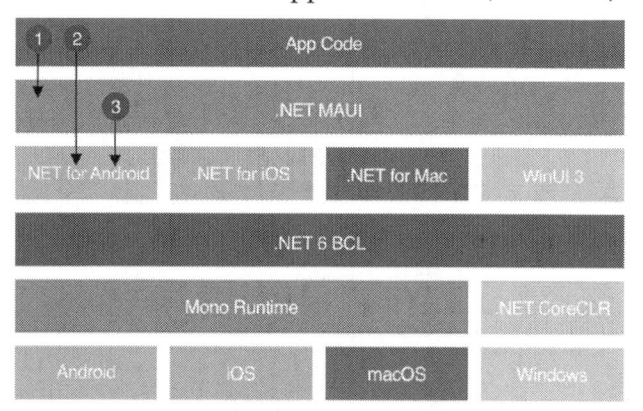

Figure 7.3: .Net MAUI Architecture

To create a .Net App, you will have to start by (1), write the code that interacts with the .Net MAUI API, then the framework will consume the native platform APIs (3) and App Code can directly connect to platform APIs if needed (2).

You can write your .Net MAUI application on a PC or Mac, and it can be compiled into the following native packages:

- **Android:** Which will compile, on application launch, from C# into intermediate language, using **Just In Time (JIT)** compiler, to a native assembly.

- **iOS:** Which will compile from C# into native ARM assembly code, fully AOT (Ahead Of Time).

- **macOS:** Which will use Mac Catalyst, an Apple solution that turns iOS apps that use UIKit into desktop app, and enhances it adding, if needed, AppKit and platform APIs.

- **Windows:** Which will use Windows UI 3 library to create native desktop apps.

.Net MAUI will also provide a set of controls to be used for data display, actions initiation, activity indication, collections displaying, data picking, and the like. Besides this, it will also provide:

- A Layout engine for page designing.
- Multiple page types that will allow creation of different navigation types.
- Data binding support to make more elegant and maintainable development patterns.
- Possibility to customize handlers, so that it will improve the way UI elements are showed.
- Several cross-platform APIs that will allow access to native device features.
- Cross-platform graphics functionality so you can be able to draw and paint shapes and images, compose operations, and transform graphical objects, using a canvas.
- Single project system that can multi target different platforms (Android, iOS, macOS and Windows).
- .Net hot reload, which will allow to modify the XAML and the managed source code, even when the app is running, being able to see it in real time, without having to rebuild the app.

New functionalities in .Net MAUI

Now, let us navigate to .Net 7 and check the new functionalities that .Net MAUI brings.

Maps

In .Net 7, .Net MAUI includes a Map control to be added to the project with a NuGet package: `Microsoft.Maui.Controls.Maps`. This is an ideal control to add an application, so it can display maps, and allow making annotations, using the native maps from each mobile platform. It will also let you draw shapes on the map, add custom pins, drop pins, and geocode street addresses, also with latitude and longitude. So, to use the control you must add the NuGet package and initialize the control in the **MauiProgram** builder, by adding **.UseMauiMaps()**, and adding to the view, the **Map** control.

We will now share code samples on how to add the Map Control and initialize it.

To add the control, you can use the following code:

```
1. <Grid>
2.     <Map x:Name="map"/>
3. </Grid>
```

And, to initialize it, you can use something like this:

```
1.  protected override void OnNavigatedTo
        (NavigatedToEventArgs args)
2.  {
3.      base.OnNavigatedTo(args);
4.
5.      var mauiLoc= new Location(20.84242,  -156.32949);
6.
7.      MapSpan mapSpan = MapSpan.FromCenterAndRadius
        (mauiLoc, Distance.FromKilometers(3));
8.      map.MoveToRegion(mapSpan);
9.      map.Pins.Add(new Pin
10.     {
11.         Label = "Welcome to .NET MAUI!",
12.         Location = mauiLoc,
13.     });
14. }
```

Desktop improvements

.Net MAUI can be used to target desktop platforms so, to improve the needs of that, Microsoft added a few useful features. It is expected that these could improve the desktop experience by including the possibility to add context menus, tooltips, pointer gestures, right-click **mapping on tap gestures** and giving more control over the window size.

In *Figure 7.4*, taken from Microsoft Devblogs, we can see an example of the context menu, with the ability to select font type.

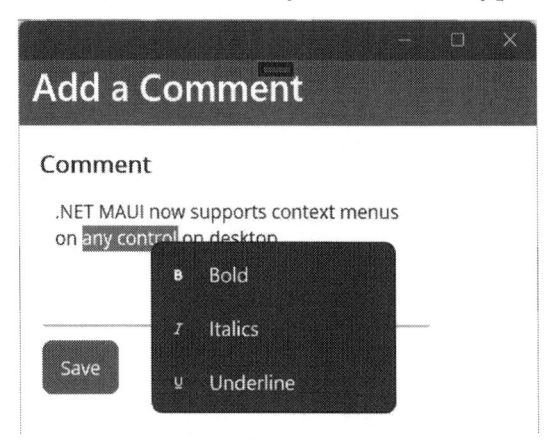

Figure 7.4: *.Net MAUI Context Menu for Desktop*

Regarding **Context Menus**, it is now possible to attach it to any visual element using the **MenuFlyout** control. This will add the options, that can be defined, as it is shown in the code below (also taken from Microsoft DevBlogs), and that will appear in the location where the user right-clicks that view, when run on a desktop platform:

1. `<Editor Text="This is my text and I want bold.">`
2. `    <FlyoutBase.ContextFlyout>`
3. `        <MenuFlyout>`
4. `            <MenuFlyoutItem Text="Bold" Clicked="OnBoldClicked"/>`
5. `            <MenuFlyoutItem Text="Italics" Clicked="OnItalicsClicked"/>`
6. `            <MenuFlyoutItem Text="Underline" Clicked="OnUnderlineClicked"/>`
7. `        </MenuFlyout>`
8. `    </FlyoutBase.ContextFlyout>`
9. `</Editor>`

Another new feature that is now added are **Tooltips** that can appear when the user hovers the cursor over an element on the screen, showing some details about that element. Now it is possible to add this feature, by adding a simple attached property on which the text that will be displayed will be set. Also, the appearance and disappearance of the tooltip will be triggered automatically.

Next, is shown another code sample, taken from Microsoft DevBlogs:

```
1.  <RadioButton Value="home"
2.      ToolTipProperties.Text="Home"
3.      SemanticProperties.DescriptionText="Home menu item">
4.      <RadioButton.Content>
5.          <Image Source="home.png"/>
6.      </RadioButton.Content>
7.  </RadioButton>
```

Also, Desktop applications will have a few **Gestures** that are different from the ones used in mobile applications, so .Net 7 brings:

- A pointer gesture for handling hover events, as seen in this example, from Microsoft DevBlogs:

```
<PointerGestureRecognizer PointerEntered="HoverBegan" PointerExited="HoverEnded" PointerMoved="HoverMoved" />
```

- A button mask for right-click taps, as it is shown following, on the code sample, also from Microsoft DevBlogs:

```
1.  var secondaryClick = new TapGestureRecognizer()
2.  {
3.      Buttons = ButtonsMask.Secondary
4.  };
5.
6.  secondaryClick.Tapped += SecondaryClick_Tapped;
```

Another feature that is now added to .Net 7 are some properties and events that control, at the cross-platform layer, the **Window Size** and **Position**, which include:

- X/Y Position – not supported on macOS
- Width/Height – not supported on macOS
- Minimum Width/Height
- Maximum Width/Height
- SizeChanged

So, to simply position and set the size of your window, here is an example from Microsoft DevBlogs, on how we can do it now:

```
1. const int newWidth = 800;
2. const int newHeight = 600;
3.
4. // get screen size
5. var disp = DeviceDisplay.Current.MainDisplayInfo;
6.
7. // center the window
8. Window.X = (disp.Width / disp.Density - newWidth) / 2;
9. Window.Y = (disp.Height / disp.Density - newHeight) / 2;
10.
11. // resize
12. Window.Width = newWidth;
13. Window.Height = newHeight;
```

Using .Net MAUI in a .Net 7 application

Well, now that we know what is and what is new for .Net MAUI let's see how we can create an app with it:

1. Open Visual Studio 2022, select **Create a New Project** and then select **MAUI** in **All project Types** dropdown and then **.Net MAUI App**. After that click **Next**, as shown in *Figure 7.5*:

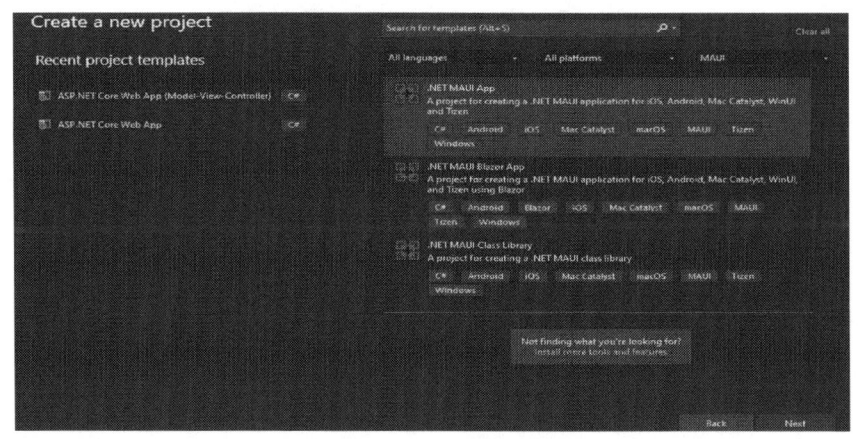

Figure 7.5: Create a .Net MAUI App

2. Set the **Project Name** and **Location** and click **Next**, as seen in *Figure 7.6*:

Figure 7.6: Configure your Net MAUI project

3. In the **Additional Information** window, click the **create** Button and then wait for the project to be created and the dependencies to be restored, as seen in the following figure:

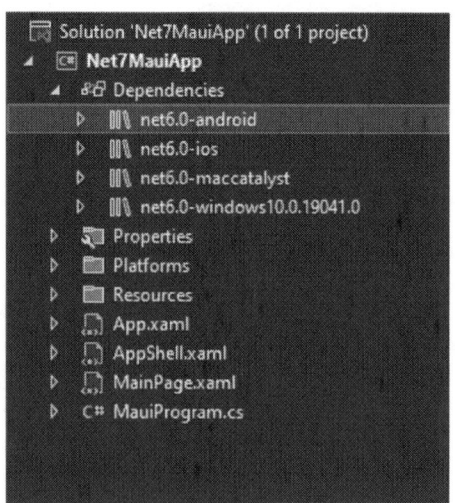

Figure 7.7: Net7MauiApp and restored dependencies

Working with .NET MAUI ■ 93

4. Then, select the **Debug Target** dropdown and select **Android Emulators | Android Emulator**, as following:

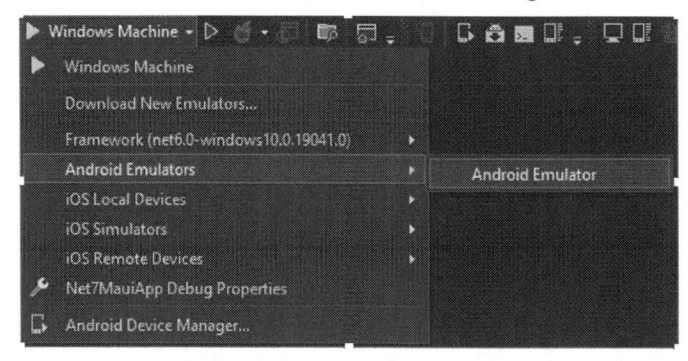

Figure 7.8: Select the Debug Target

5. Press the **Android Emulator** button, which will start to install the Android SDK and **Android Emulator**. The first step is to **Accept** the Android SDK – **License Agreement**, as seen in the following figure:

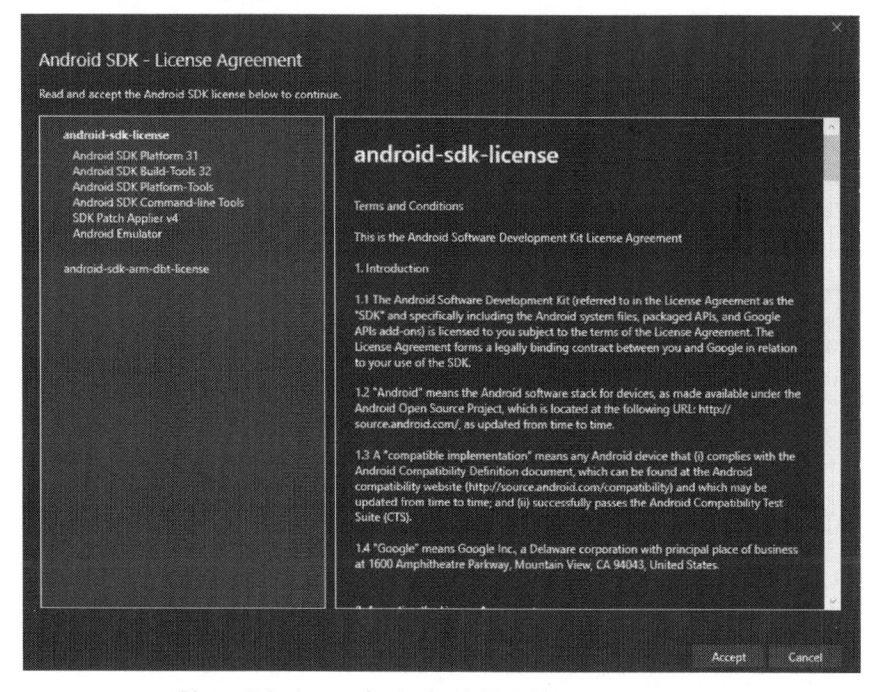

Figure 7.9: Accept the Android SDK License Agreement

6. Afterwards, you must allow the app to make changes to your device, like is shown in *Figure 7.10*:

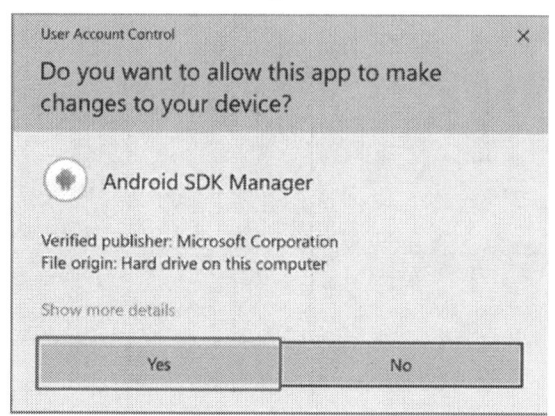

***Figure 7.10**: Allow the app to make changes to your device*

7. Then, in the **New Device** window, select the **Create** button, so that a Default Android Device is created, as it is shown in *Figure 7.11*:

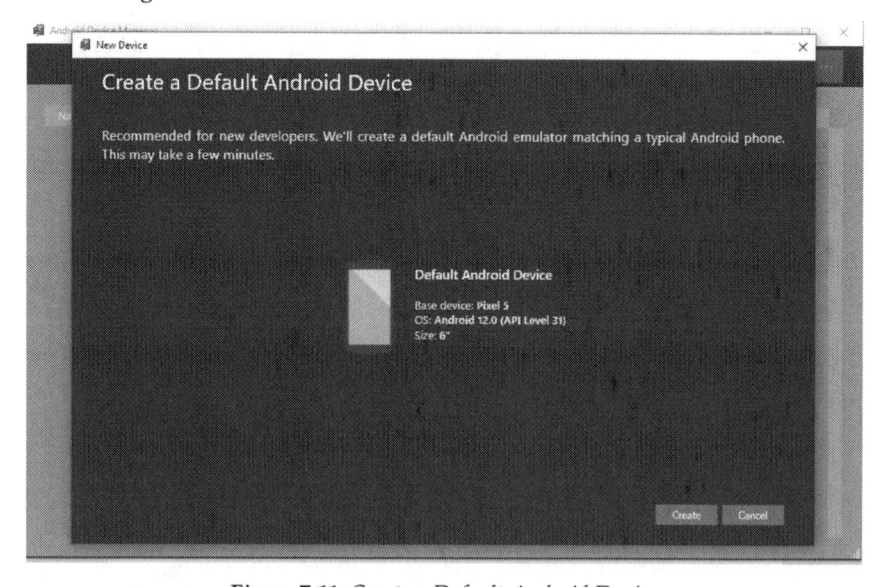

***Figure 7.11**: Create a Default Android Device*

8. Wait for Visual Studio to download and create the emulator, and then close the **Android Device Manager** window, it is as seen in *Figure 7.12*:

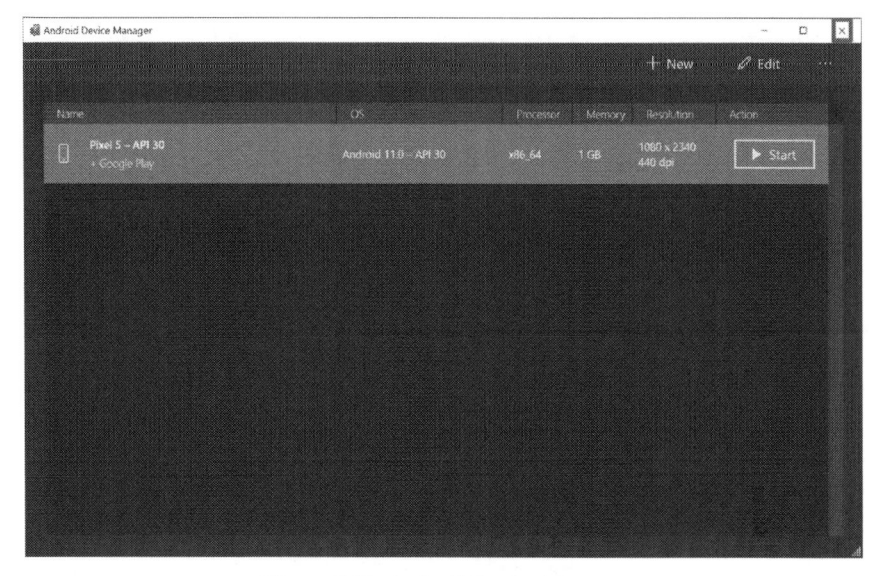

Figure 7.12: Android Device Manager

9. It will generate a Debug Target named "Pixel 5 – API 30 (Android 11.0 – API 30)". You can then click on that button to build and run the app, and the app will be shown as seen in *Figure 7.13*:

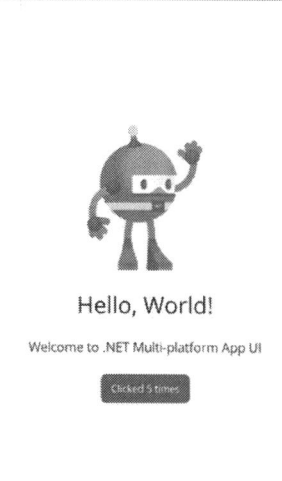

Figure 7.13: Debug and Run Android App

Different libraries and platform specific frameworks

For platform integration, .Net MAUI has some specific frameworks that are needed for different platforms.

One of the platforms that needs specific functionalities is **iOS**.

So, for **iOS**, .Net MAUI brings the following platform-specific functionalities:

- **For views:**
    - Setting the Cell background colour
    - Controlling item selection occurrence in a DatePicker, in a Picker and in a TimePicker
    - Adjust the font size to ensure that inputted text fits into an Entry
    - Setting cursor colour in an Entry
    - Control if a ListView header cell will float during scroll
    - When updating ListView items collection, control if row animations are disabled
    - Setting separator style in ListView
    - Control if SearchBar will have background
    - Enable Slider.Value property to be set when tapping on one Slider bar position, instead of dragging the Slider thumbnail
    - Control transitions used when opening SwipeView
- **For pages:**
    - Control the shadow applied to the detail page of a FlyoutPage
    - Control if the Navigation Bar is translucent
    - Control, in page navigation bar, if the page title is shown as a large title
    - Set the presentation style for modal pages
    - Set if a tab bar on a TabbedPage is translucent

- **For layouts:**
    - Control if a ScrollView handles touch gestures or, instead, will pass it to its content
- **For application class:**
    - Enable PanGestureRecognizer in scrolling views, so it will capture and share the pan gesture when using scrolling view

And, for **Windows**, there are also some specific functionalities:

- **For views, pages, and layouts:**
    - Setting access key for a VisualElement
- **For views:**
    - Finding reading order from text content in Entry, Editor and Label instances
    - Adding the possibility for tap gesture support in a List View
    - Enabling the change of pull direction on a RefreshView
    - Enabling SearchBar interaction with spell check engine
- **For application class:**
    - Define from which directory, in the project, image assets will be loaded.

Also, for **Android**, there are some specific functionalities, which will be shown next:

- **For views:**
    - Setting input method editor options for an Entry soft keyboard
    - Enabling fast scroll in ListView
    - Control which transition will be used when opening SwipeView
    - Controlling if a WebView can display mixed content
    - Enable Zoom on WebView
- **For pages:**
    - Disable transition animations, on a TabbedPage, when navigating between the pages

- o   Enable swiping between pages, in TabbedPage
- o   Setting toolbar placement and colour in TabbedPage
- **For application class:**
  - o   Setting operating mode of soft keyboard

Conclusion

In this chapter we have learned about a new framework that Microsoft is implementing, to replace Xamarin, that is .Net Multi-platform Application User Interface (MAUI). This framework is being implemented, since .Net 6 and is getting bigger and with more improvements and utilities being brought to .Net 7.

So, we got into the detail of what .Net MAUI is, learned what is new in .Net 7 for .Net MAUI, always sharing some code samples; and learned how to use .Net MAUI in .Net 7, to create, in the case, an Android Application. But, of course, this can also be applied for other platforms, because one thing that .Net MAUI brings is the ability to have a single project that can be shared and used by different platforms.

Another final thing that we have learned here are different libraries present in each platform (macOS, iOS, Android, and Windows).

Next, we will get to know another framework that is now being improved for .Net 7, which is Blazor.

So, hope you have enjoyed this chapter and are enthusiastic about these new functionalities that .Net 7 brings, and with them great possibilities to improve and simplify a developers work, and with it being able to deliver better solutions!

Now, relax a bit, and prepare for the next ride.

Join our book's Discord space

Join the book's Discord Workspace for Latest updates, Offers, Tech happenings around the world, New Release and Sessions with the Authors:

https://discord.bpbonline.com

CHAPTER 8
Blazor in .NET 7

Introduction

We are heading fast and halfway through our journey.

After having visited the realms of .Net MAUI, we will now discover another framework that was released in .Net 6 and is now being improved: Blazor.

We will first learn what is Blazor, and what it is for. Blazor, as we will see, is connected to the improvements and developments being made on .Net MAUI.

So, another thing that we will travel to and discover a bit more is what is new for Blazor, in .Net 7 and get to know a bit of Blazor Hybrid.

We will see how it will allow to share code and libraries and interact with JavaScript Interop.

Hope you are ready for this journey as this will be quite a ride.

To prepare let us feast our eyes with Blazor logo, in *Figure 8.1*:

Figure 8.1: Blazor Logo.

Structure

The topics that will be covered in this chapter will be:

- What is Blazor
- An introduction to Blazor in .Net 7
- A Bit on Blazor Hybrid
- Share code and libraries
- JavaScript Interop

Objectives

This chapter has the objective of learning more about this new feature, presented in .Net 6, that is used to build interactive User Interfaces, using C#, instead of JavaScript: Blazor.

We will see what this really is, get to know what .Net 7 brings new and learn some specifics about it: a bit on Blazor hybrid, share code and libraries and JavaScript Interop.

An introduction to Blazor in .Net 7

First, let us understand what is Blazor? It is a feature of ASP.Net that extends its framework, with tools and libraries for building web apps, and interactive web **User Interfaces** (**UIs**), using C# instead of JavaScript. These apps are composed of reusable web UI components, implemented in C#, HTML, and CSS. It will let you write C# code both on client and server side, so that it can be easy to share the code and libraries.

Blazor can be executed directly in the browser, running there the client-side, using WebAssembly. Due to this, you can re-use and share code and libraries from server-side parts of your application.

Blazor WebAssembly (also abbreviated as WASM) is a single-page app framework that is used to build interactive client-side web apps using .Net. It is optimized for fast download and maximum execution speed and is supported in browsers without the need for plugins.

Its code can fully access browser functionalities, using JavaScript interops – as we will see ahead. The code that is executed using WebAssembly will run in browser's JavaScript sandbox, being protected against malicious actions coming from the client's machine.

In *Figure 8.2*, we can see the schema of WebAssembly interaction between Blazor and the browser:

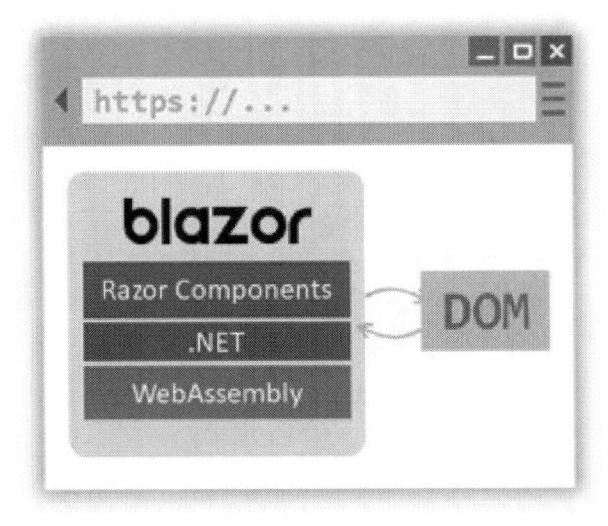

Figure 8.2: Blazor WebAssembly

Running a Blazor WebAssembly app in the browser will allow C# code files and Razor files compilation into **.Net** assemblies, these assemblies and .Net Runtimes will be downloaded to the browser, .Net runtime will configure the runtime load assemblies from the application. It will use JavaScript Interop to handle **Document Object Model (DOM**) manipulation and browser API calls.

Using Blazor WebAssembly will also reduce download times for large applications, optimizing the payload size because it will:

- Remove unused code from the app, when it is published (using Intermediate Language – IL - Trimmer).
- Compress HTTP responses.
- Cache in the browser .Net runtime and assemblies.

But, if you want, you can still run your client logic on the server. The events from Client User Interface are sent back to the server using SignalR – which we will learn about up ahead in one of the next chapters. In the following figure, taken from Microsoft Learn website, we can see the communication between the browser and Blazor server, using SignalR:

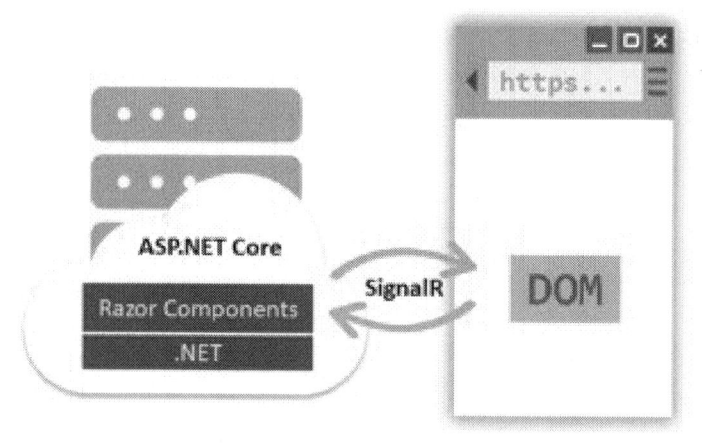

Figure 8.3: Blazor Server <-> Browser Communication with SignalR

A Blazor application is based on components, which are elements of the user interface like Pages, Dialogs or Data Entry Forms, for example.

These components are C# classes built into .Net assemblies that will define flexible UI rendering logic and handle user events. These components can be nested and reused and, shared and distributed as Razor class libraries or NuGet packages.

Usually, when we create the components class, we write it as a **Razor** markup page, using `.razor` file extension. Razor combines HTML markup and C# code and allows the switch between these two languages in the same file with Intellisense programming in Visual Studio.

Components, despite using Razor, are different from the ones used in Razor Pages and MVC, because these ones are used specifically for client-side User Interface logic and composition.

New in Blazor for .Net 7

Now we know what Blazor is, it is time to see what is new in .Net 7. So, Blazor will bring some new features, to improve and tweak what has been made in .Net 6.

It will have a new WebAssembly loading page and improvements in data binding and virtualization.

We will now check the different improvements that will be visible in this .Net version.

- **WebAssembly**

    It will have a new UI construct, which will show the progress of loading and app.

    o Two new CSS custom properties, which will act as variables, will change the loading screen animation. These CSS properties are now part of Blazor WebAssembly, which represents the client-side component of Blazor. They will show:

    - The percentage of app files loaded.
    - The percentage of app files loaded rounded to the nearest whole number.

    In the following figure, it will show an example of this new CSS loading page:

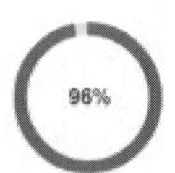

Figure 8.4: Blazor CSS loading page

- **Data binding**
    - In .Net 7, Blazor has a new and improved way of binding between UI elements or component parameters and .Net objects.
    - It was created a new **@bind:after** modifier to allow a developer to execute async code after the completion of binding events.
    - The binding between component parameters and underlying UI elements are also improved and simplified, by adding two new modifiers: **@bind:get** and **@bind:set**.
- **Virtualize**
    - The **Virtualize** component is used to limit UI render to the currently visible parts. This can be very helpful when there is a long list of items to be rendered and only a few are visible. It will use a spacer element so it can define vertical height of the scroll region enclosed in **div** element by default.
    - In .Net 7, it was added the possibility to configure a new **SpacerElement** parameter, for the cases the parent element does not allow child **div** elements. This new **SpacerElement** will be then used to configure the spacer used by **Virtualize**.
- **Navigation**
    - In .Net 7 it is now possible to pass state when navigating using **NavigationManager**. This will enable simple communication between different pages.
    - It will be introduced a new **LocationChanging** event to implement logic that occurs before navigation takes place.
- **Templates**
    - In .Net 7, Microsoft will make some small changes to the existing Blazor templates, to simplify the structure and redesign the themes.
    - Also, it will be implemented an empty Template, simpler than the existing ones, with less pre-existing code and UI.

A Bit on Blazor Hybrid

Blazor Hybrid is a way to build interactive client-side web User Interface with .Net in an ASP .NET Core application. This will allow blending desktop and mobile native client frameworks with .Net.

In an application of this type, Razor components will run on the device and render to an embedded Web View control using a local interop channel. The components will not run in Browser and WebAssembly will not be used. This will make Razor components to be loaded quickly and code to be executed faster. Also, components will have full access to native capabilities of the device, using .Net.

Blazor Hybrid will be interconnected with .Net MAUI framework. .Net MAUI includes **BlazorWebView** control to render Razor Components into an embedded Web View. With this connection, it will be possible to reuse one set of web UI components across different platforms.

Figure 8.5 shows how with the way Blazor and .Net MAUI will be combined:

Figure 8.5: *Blazor Hybrid and .Net MAUI*

It will then be able to Reuse User Interface components in native and through different platforms, Mix and Match Web and Native User Interfaces, access directly to native device functionalities, create cross-platform mobile and desktop apps.

Besides .Net MAUI, Blazor Hybrid apps can be built with **Windows Presentation Foundation_(WPF)** and **Windows Forms**, by using **BlazorWebView** controls. Razor components will run natively in

Windows and then render to an embedded Web View. Using Blazor in these two platforms, will allow the addition of new User Interfaces to the existing Windows Desktop apps, and reuse it across platforms, integrating with .Net MAUI or on the web.

To use Blazor Hybrid Web View configuration for different platforms, it will be needed to configure `BlazorWebView` control using the following events:

- `BlazorWebViewInitializing`: It gives access to settings used to create Web Views for each platform.
- `BlazorWebViewInitialized`: It gives access to make additional setting configurations on Web Views.

Sharing code and libraries

Blazor will use .Net Standard so that these projects can reference the existing .Net libraries and Standard specifications.

These libraries can be shared across different .Net platforms and are used to integrate Blazor with .Net MAUI, for example. Other platforms that share these libraries with Blazor are .Net Core, Mono and Unity. For those who do not know, Unity is one of the largest cross-platform game engine. It was first released in June 2005 and is very popular on indie game development. It is used for developing games for several platforms, such as, Mobile (iOs, Android), Desktop (Windows, Mac, Linux), Consoles (PS4, PS5, Xbox, Nintendo Switch, Stadia) and also for Virtual Reality platforms like Oculus, Playstation VR, Google's ARCore and much more. As an example of video games that uses Unity are Pokemon Go or Call of Duty. Unity can also be used for other than video games and is now being used in films and automotive market.

If some of these APIs are not applicable inside of a web browser, it will be thrown a PlatformNotSupportedException.

JavaScript Interop

A Blazor application can interact with JavaScript, by invoking its functions, from .Net methods and can have .Net methods invoked by JavaScript functions.

This is what we call JavaScript Interop (interoperability). In the following figure it is a representation, taken from Microsoft DotNet site, which shows this communication:

Figure 8.6: Javascript Interop communication with C# Blazor app

Blazor will only interact with unmodified document object model elements. If an element is modified by JavaScript, it can result in undefined behaviour in Blazor, because it will no longer match its internal representation.

JavaScript calls are asynchronous by default so that they are compatible with Blazor hosting models, Blazor Servers and Blazer WebAssembly. If you are using Blazor Server, the asynchrony must be used since the calls are sent over network connection. The only way to use synchronous JavaScript Interop calls is to use Blazor WebAssembly hosting.

For serialization, Blazor will use **System.Text.Json** with these requirements and behaviours:

- A default constructor must always exist for types, get-set must be public, and fields cannot be serialized.
- You cannot customize global default serialization, because if you do, you can break existing component libraries, impact on performance and security and reduce reliability.
- If you serialize .Net member names, it will then result in lowercase JSON key names
- When you deserialize JSON, you will get JsonElement C# instances. This will allow mixed casting. Even when there are case differences between JSON key names and C# property names, internal casting for assignment to C# model properties, will work as expected, due to this mixed casing. Next is an example, taken from Microsoft Learn, where you can see how JSON can be deserialized:

```csharp
1.  using System.Text.Json;
2.
3.  namespace DeserializeExtra
4.  {
5.      public class WeatherForecast
6.      {
7.          public DateTimeOffset Date { get; set; }
8.          public int TemperatureCelsius { get; set; }
9.          public string? Summary { get; set; }
10.         public string? SummaryField;
11.         public IList<DateTimeOffset>? DatesAvailable { get; set; }
12.         public Dictionary<string, HighLowTemps>? TemperatureRanges { get; set; }
13.         public string[]? SummaryWords { get; set; }
14.     }
15.
16.     public class HighLowTemps
17.     {
18.         public int High { get; set; }
19.         public int Low { get; set; }
20.     }
21.
22.     public class Program
23.     {
24.         public static void Main()
25.         {
26.             string jsonString =
27.                 @"{
28.                     ""Date"": ""2019-08-01T00:00:00-07:00"",
29.                     ""TemperatureCelsius"": 25,
30.                     ""Summary"": ""Hot"",
31.                     ""DatesAvailable"": [
32.                     ""2019-08-01T00:00:00-07:00"",
33.                     ""2019-08-02T00:00:00-07:00""
```

```
34.                                    ],
35.             """TemperatureRanges""": {
36.                       """Cold""": {
37.                         """High""": 20,
38.                         """Low""": -10
39.                                    },
40.                        """Hot""": {
41.                         """High""": 60,
42.                         """Low""": 20
43.                                    }
44.                                    },
45.             """SummaryWords""": [
46.                                """Cool""",
47.                                """Windy""",
48.                                """Humid"""
49.                                ]
50.             }
51.             ";
52.
53.         WeatherForecast? weatherForecast =
54.             JsonSerializer.Deserialize
    <WeatherForecast>(jsonString);
55.
56.         Console.
    WriteLine($"Date: {weatherForecast?.Date}");
57.         Console.
    WriteLine($"TemperatureCelsius: {weatherForecast?.
    TemperatureCelsius}");
58.         Console.
    WriteLine($"Summary: {weatherForecast?.Summary}");
59.     }
60. }
61. }
62. // output:
63. //Date: 8/1/2019 12:00:00 AM -07:00
64. //TemperatureCelsius: 25
65. //Summary: Hot
```

.Net 7 will bring, expectedly, support for **System.DateOnly** and **System.TimeOnly**.

Blazor can be used in optimized Byte array JavaScript Interop, which avoids encoding and decoding byte arrays into Base64.

Another useful tool used by Blazor, before and after app loading are JavaScript Initializers. They are especially useful for customizing Blazor app way of loading, initializing libraries before Blazor starts and configuring Blazor settings. These JavaScript Initializers are detected as part of the build process and then, automatically imported in Blazor applications.

To define the JavaScript Initializer, we must add a JavaScript module to the project, giving it the name **[assembly name\library name\ package identifier].lib.module.js**. The file must be stored in the **wwwroot** folder of the project. This module will then export one or both functions:

- **beforeStart(options, extensions)**: User to customize the loading process, logging process and some other options specific to the hosting model, and is called before Blazor starts.
    - If it is used in Blazor WebAssembly, it can also specify the use of custom boot resource loader.
    - If used in Blazor Sever it will receive SignalR start options.
    - In BlazorWebViews, it will not receive any options.
- **afterStarted**: Used to initialize libraries calling JavaScript interop and registering custom elements and is called after Blazor is ready to receive JavaScript calls.

Blazor also enables JavaScript isolation in standard JavaScript modules, which will bring the following benefits:

- Cleaner global namespace because it will not have Imported JavaScript to "pollute" it.
- It does not need the consumption of libraries and components to import the related JavaScript.

Conclusion

In this chapter we have learned about another framework brought in .Net 6 and now being tweaked and improved for .Net 7: Blazor.

Blazor, as we have seen in the first part of the chapter, when we have learned what it is, is a feature of .Net that extends its framework and helps the building of web apps and interactive Web User Interfaces with the use of C# instead of JavaScript. It will also be connected to the improvements made on .Net MAUI.

After learning what Blazor is, we have stepped into the next page and learned what are the improvements and changes that it will bring in .Net 7.

Also, there is another cool thing that we have travelled to, which was Blazor Hybrid, which is the part where we have connected with the previous chapter, because it is intertwined with .Net MAUI.

Finally, we have gone into the part of code sharing and libraries, and checked how Blazor can interact with JavaScript Interop, easing up its usage.

So, after this, it is now time for us to relax, take a deep breath and prepare for the next chapter, on which we will continue learning about .Net world and this .Net 7 version, with its improvements and ease of work.

In the next chapter will see us go through another interesting bit, which is creating a desktop user interface. After seeing how .Net MAUI and Blazor work, it is now time to check another way of creating this.

Hope you are ready and enjoying the ride. There is still a lot to go through.

Join our book's Discord space

Join the book's Discord Workspace for Latest updates, Offers, Tech happenings around the world, New Release and Sessions with the Authors:

https://discord.bpbonline.com

CHAPTER 9
Creating a Desktop UI

Introduction

What a great journey till now! After learning about .Net MAUI and Blazor it is now time to combine them a bit and learn how to build desktop UI applications.

We will start by getting to know what a desktop UI is and after that, how we can implement and create one. We will go through some topics we have seen before, like .Net MAUI and Blazor Hybrid, but also getting to know a bit on Windows Forms - and how to create a WinForms app.

Also, we will go through **Windows UI (WinUI)** library – used by .Net MAUI - and Windows App SDK. Hope you will enjoy this next step in this chapter through the realms of .Net 7.

Enjoy the following figure, taken from Microsoft DotNet page, showing our little friend DotNetBot creating desktop apps.

Figure 9.1: Desktop Apps

Structure

The topics that will be covered in this chapter will be:

- What is a desktop UI
- How to implement and create it
- Use WinForms

Objectives

This chapter has the objective of learning more about desktop UI and how to create them. After getting to know what the capabilities of .Net MAUI and Blazor are, we will know go back to the desktop applications and learn a bit more about them and go through some new topics like Windows Forms (although this is something that already exists in past versions).

Desktop UI

As we have seen before, in previous chapter, we can create applications for different platforms.

So, we can use .Net MAUI as a multi-platform application but if we solely want to create an application that runs on our native desktop computer, we can create a desktop UI.

Desktop UI is the user interface for a desktop application. What is a desktop application, you may ask. Well, it is an application that executes in our desktop computer and normally is installed directly on it.

If you are creating an application that you are going to run only on Windows, Microsoft recommends that a desktop application is created, and to do so you can use Windows App SDK and WinUI 3. If you need it to run on multiple platforms, you can go to the latest chapters and create this application, using .Net MAUI or even Blazor Hybrid.

WinUI 3

Now, let us look at Win UI 3. What is this?

Win UI stands for Windows User Interface, and it is a framework library used for Windows desktop apps. The version 3, that we are covering here is the latest one and recommended for usage with .Net 7.

This framework is available as part of Windows App SDK – which is a set of developer components and tools for application development. The Windows App SDK gives a set of APIs and tools to be used by any C++ Win32 or C# .Net application, for several Windows Operating System versions.

Windows User Interface can also be used as basis for cross-platform technologies, like .Net MAUI. This will join the power of WinUI on Windows applications and will enable execution on other operating systems.

Figure 9.2 is a figure of WinUI library logo:

Figure 9.2: *WinUI logo*

WinUI on .Net MAUI

As seen before, .Net MAUI is a powerful tool that allows building cross-platform applications to be used in Android, iOS, macOS and

Windows. This framework will improve the native UI and services of each platform, using a single .Net Code Base.

So, to do this, .Net MAUI will use platform native experience, and WinUI 3 and Windows App SDK, to guarantee that applications have the latest user experience on Windows. With these abilities, the apps created in .Net MAUI will have access to all the tools available in WinUI 3 and the ability to be disponible to other platforms.

Although we had a chapter dedicated to .Net MAUI let us refresh the knowledge and review what it will be a great choice for:

- Sharing as much .Net code as possible across mobile and desktop applications
- Take your application to other desktop and mobile targets with native platform experiences, instead of sticking only to Windows
- Use C# and XAML to build cross-platform applications
- Using Blazor in Web development and including all or part of it in mobile or desktop applications (Blazor Hybrid)

Other desktop applications - Win32

Win32 applications are the classic desktop applications, used for native Windows applications that require direct access to Windows and hardware. So, it will be the choice if you want a high performant application that can directly access system hardware.

Win32 API will use C++ to improve performance and efficiency by controlling target platform with unmanaged code running on managed runtime environment like WinRT and .Net. It will also require that you will need great care and attention to get everything right.

This API will enable building high-performance applications because it uses:

- Optimizations on hardware level, like resources allocation, object lifetimes, data layout, alignment, and the like.
- Access to performance-oriented instruction sets.
- Templates to improve efficiency and type-safe generic programming.

- Containers and algorithms that are safe and more efficient.
- Direct3D.
- Windows runtime to create the apps with first-class access to its APIs.

Other desktop applications – Windows Forms

This is the original UI model for desktop applications. It is a simple and lightweight platform that gives access to .Net Framework. It allows quick development, even when you are new to the platform. It is forms-based and have a lot of built-in visual and non-visual drag and drop controls, which, as said, will manage the development to be easier and faster. Windows forms will not use XAML but will use WinUI 3.

Creating a WinUI 3 project

Now, let us see how we can use Visual Studio to create a WinUI3 desktop project. We will look at some code and how it works.

So, first you need to open Visual Studio, and then **File | New | Project**. Select C#, Windows and WinUI on the dropdowns that appear in the new project dialog, as seen in the following figure:

Figure 9.3: Select data to create a new WinUI project

Then you can select **Blank App, packaged (Win UI 3 in Desktop)** project template, and click **Next**, as seen in *Figure 9.4*:

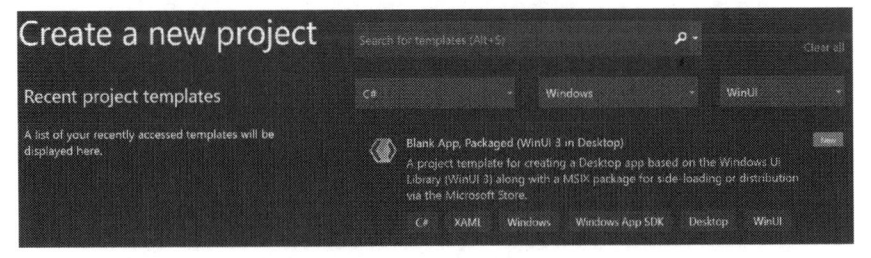

Figure 9.4: Project Template for New WinUI 3 project

118 ■ .NET 7 for Jobseekers

Afterwards, you must insert a project name, and a folder, and then click **Create**. It will create an `App.xaml` file and code-behind files that represent the running application, and a `MainWindow.xaml` file with its respective code-behind files that will be the main window displayed by the application.

In the following figure, is an example of the `MainWindow.xaml` and the solution explorer:

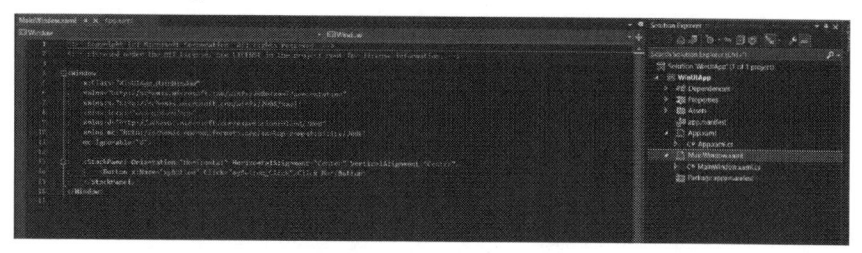

Figure 9.5: MainWindow.xaml

If you want to add new items to your application, you need to right-click on the project in **Solution Explorer**, then select **Add | New Item**, as seen in the following figure:

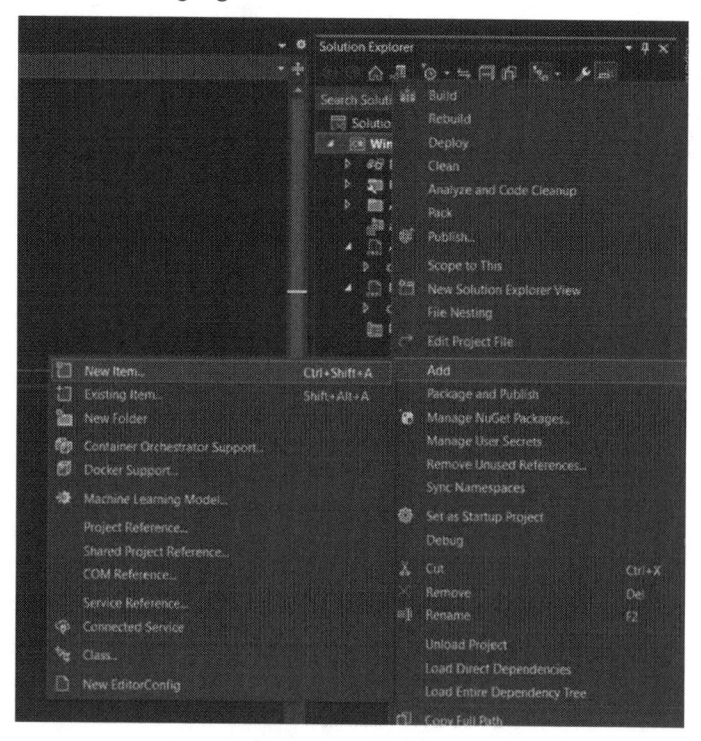

Figure 9.6: Add New Item

Creating a Desktop UI ■ 119

On the dialog that appears, select **WinUI**, choose the item you will add, rename it and click **add**, as seen in *Figure 9.7*:

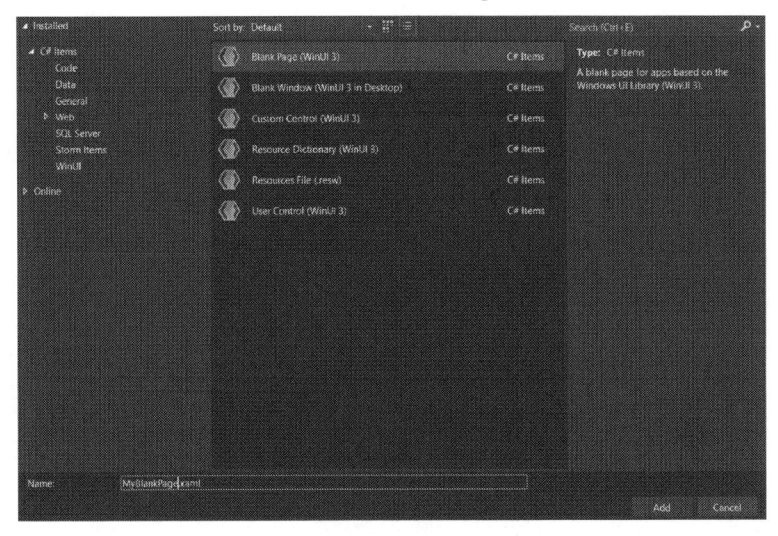

Figure 9.7: Choose WinUI and add item

Then you can build and run the application, to validate if it is correct and without errors.

Note that, in order to run the application, you will have to activate developer mode on Windows.

When running the application, you will get a screen like the one shown in the following figure:

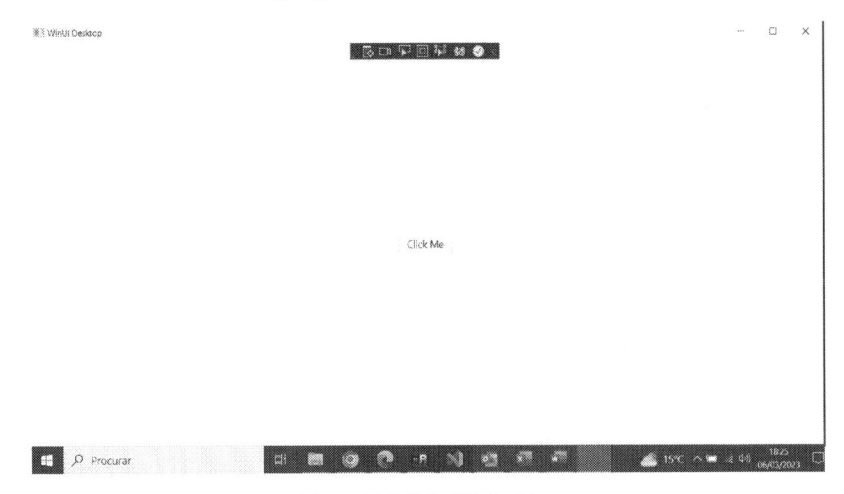

Figure 9.8: WinUI Desktop

120 ▪ .NET 7 for Jobseekers

When you click the button, it will change its own content (text) from "**Click Me**" to "**Clicked**" as seen in *Figure 9.9*:

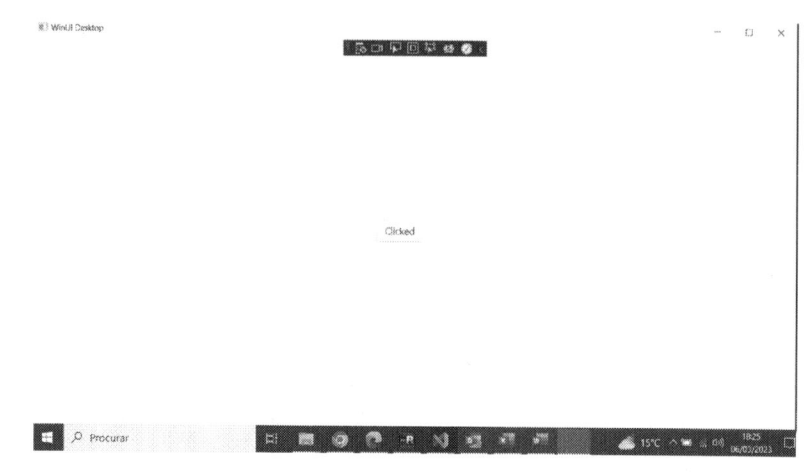

Figure 9.9: WinUI Desktop after interaction with button

Now, let us look at the code that we have used.

It will contain the entry point, which is the main function. This entry point will be the step where Windows will start our application. Normally this is a hidden function auto generated by Visual Studio, when creating a new project, so you do not have to worry about it.

We will also have a class that represents the application as a whole, which is typically **App.xaml** class, which is a class that derives from WinUI 3 **Microsoft.UI.Xaml.Application** class.

Figure 9.10 that shows an example of this class:

Figure 9.10: App.xaml

This xaml will work the following way:

- The code generated in the entry point creates an instance of **App**, so it can run
- In **App** constructor, there is a call to **InitializeComponent**, which will parse the content of the XAML markup, in order to merge resources so they can be resolved and loaded into a dictionary to be used by the running application.
- **App** also have **OnLaunched** method that creates and activates a new instance of the **MainWindow**.

We can see these methods in *Figure 9.11*.

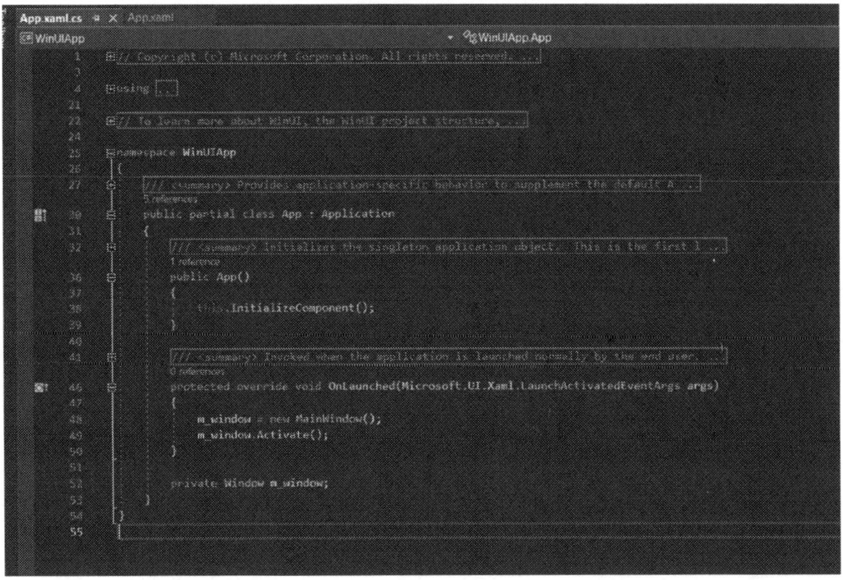

Figure 9.11: App.xaml codebehind

This **MainWindow.xaml** class will represent the main window that will be displayed by the application. This is a class that derives from WinUI 3 **Microsoft.UI.Xaml.Window** class.

122 ■ .NET 7 for Jobseekers

In the following figure, it is a representation of this class:

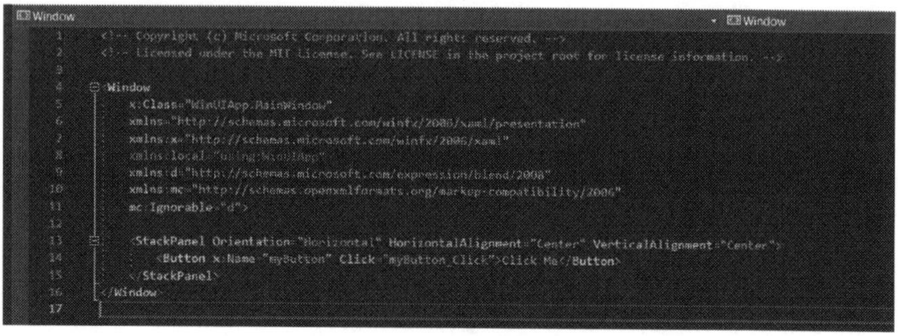

Figure 9.12: MainWindow.xaml

Also, as seen before, this class will have a constructor that calls the **InitializeComponent** method, which will turn the XAML markup into a **User Interface** (**UI**) object.

This xaml will contain the basic layout of **MainWindow**, having at it is root a dynamic panel called **Microsoft.UI.Xaml.Controls.StackPanel**. This **StackPanel** contains a Button that connect to an event handler method for the click event, and will be of **Microsoft.UI.Xaml.Controls.Button** type.

The button will have a **myButton_Click** method that will change its content from **"Click Me"** to **"Clicked"**.

In the following figure, we can see a representation of the code behind class:

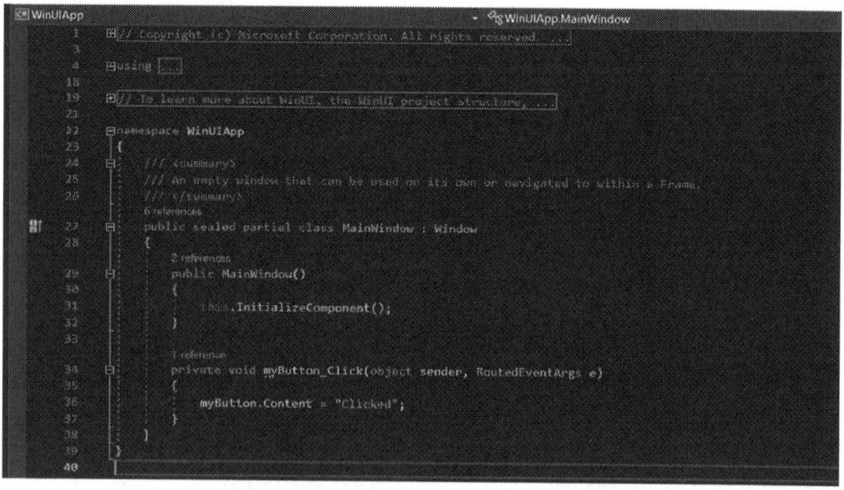

Figure 9.13: MainWindow.xaml code behind

We have also created a new **MyBlankPage.xaml** class that is shown in *Figure 9.14*. It is a simple empty class, that was created just to understand how we can add a new page to a WinUI 3 application. This is a derivation of **Microsoft.UI.Xaml.Controls.Page**.

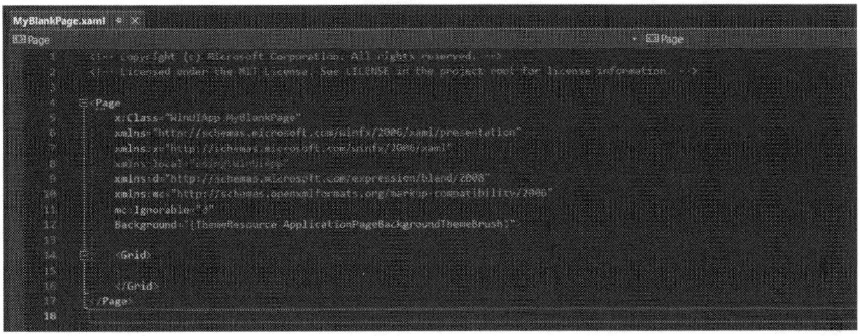

Figure 9.14: *MyBlankPage.xaml*

The code behind will only have an instantiation of **InitializeComponent** method.

In *Figure 9.15* is shown a representation of the code behind class, written in C#.

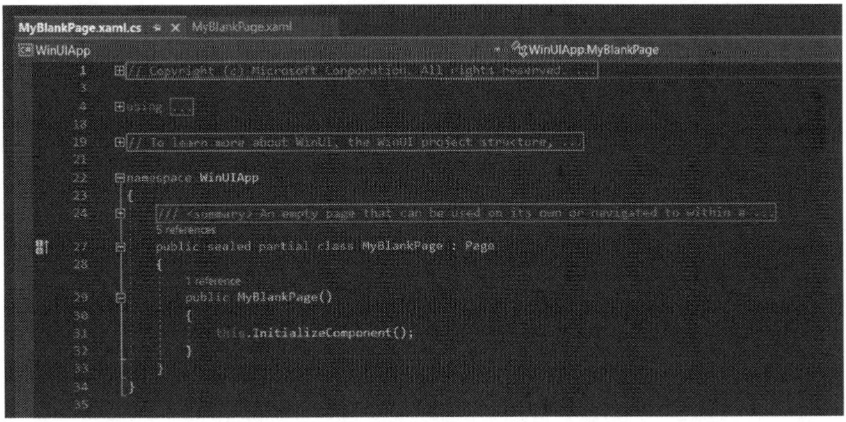

Figure 9.15: *MyBlankPage.xaml codebehind*

Windows forms improvements in .Net 7

.Net 7 will also bring some improvements to Desktop UI and applications by having some fixes and enhancements made to Windows Forms development.

It will have improvements regarding User experience and accessibility, like:

- Screen readers, for example, narrator, is now improved and more accurate when informs about the controls used. One example is **ListView** that is now correctly announced when a group is expanded or collapsed.

- There are more controls with UI Automation support: **TreeView, DateTimePicker, ToolStripContainer, ToolStripPanel, FlowLayoutPanel, TableLayoutPanel, SplitContainer, PrintPreviewControl** and **WebBrowser**.

- Fix on the memory leaks on narrator, regarding some controls and their corresponding accessible objects.

- **DataGridView, ListView, TabControl** and others now have correct bounding rectangles for nested forms and some elements of composite controls

- Correction on **ExpandCollapse** control pattern support for **ListView, TreeView** and **PropertyGrid**.

- Corrections also done on colour contrast ratio in Buttons, **PropertyGrid** and **DataGridView**

- Improvement in visibility for high-contrast themes in **ToolStripTextBox** and **ToolStripButton**

Also, DPI support and scaling in multi-monitor scenarios, have had some improvements done, in .Net 7. So, Windows forms is now able to:

- Scale nested controls, by having corrected layout issues due to different order of Windows messages in PerMonitorV2 mode. Before, a parent control will receive the message regarding **WM_DPICHANGED** after all its children, which is now fixed.

- **Form.MaximumSize** and **Form.MinimumSize** properties can now be scaled based on current monitor DPI settings, if an application is running on **ApplicationHighDpiMode**, using **PerMonitorV2**

.Net 7 now has a switch that controls the forms minimum and maximum size properties, when **WM_DPICHANGED** message is received. It is called **System.Windows.Forms.ScaleTopLevelFormMinMaxSizeForDpi**.

Another thing that is now changed, for Windows Forms, in .Net 7, is the possibility to move business logic from the form code-behind into a modern pattern like **Model-View-ViewModel (MVVM)**, so it can be easily reused and tested.

It will also include a new data binding strategy, due to the fact Visual Studio no longer supports data source provider service for .Net Runtime.

Windows forms contains a powerful binding engine, so Microsoft empowered it, by introducing support for a more modern form of data binding, using data contexts and command patters, like the ones that are used for data binding in **Windows Presentation Foundation (WPF)**

The following figure, taken from Microsoft DevBlogs, illustrates a sample of the data binding improvements:

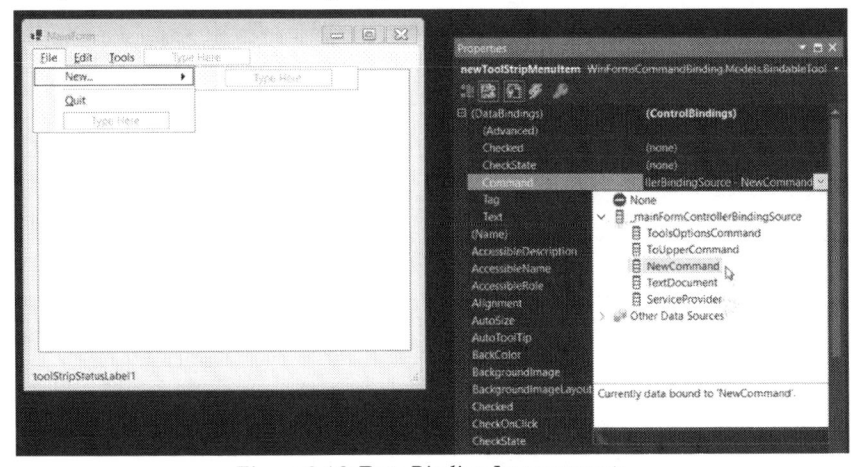

Figure 9.16: Data Binding Improvements

This will drive the Windows forms development into an MVVM pattern and simplifies the use of object-relational mappers from ViewModels. It will also allow a code reduction and simplification, in code-behind, which will lead to new testing possibilities.

Besides this, it will enable code sharing between Windows forms and other .NET UI frameworks, like WinUI, WPF or .Net MAUI.

If you want to add these new features on .Net 7 Windows form development, you need to add `<EnablePreviewFeatures>true</EnablePreviewFeatures>` to the project file (regardless of the language you use – C# or Visual Basic).

One last improvement we would like to refer is the replacement of Windows forms built-in COM interops with ComWrappers, so it will not be disabled when using native **Ahead-Of-Time (AOT)** scenarios. Ahead-Of-Time compilation is when an higher-level language is compiled into a lower-level one, usually at build-time, before execution of a program, to reduce the amount of work needed at run time. This is good, because it simplifies the ability to run code in native AOT without having to do additional customizations and allows a Windows form to run under native AOT.

Conclusion

In this chapter we have learned about desktop UI applications.

After getting to know how .Net MAUI and Blazor works, we got back into desktop and entered the world of how to use and create desktop UI applications.

We went through some points, starting to learn what a desktop UI is, how can we implement one and types of desktop UIs, like Windows forms, Win32 and of course, discussed about the usage of .Net MAUI, which will use one thing we have learned here: WinUI 3.

Regarding WinUI 3 and Windows App SDK, we have learned what they are and how to use it.

Also, another point seen in this chapter was the creation of a WinUI 3 application.

Hope you enjoyed and learned useful and interesting aspects.

Now it is time to relax a bit, before the next chapter, on which we will go through the communication with the Views of an application, we will go a bit back, into our MVC examples and learn how it will be possible to communicate with the views part.

Join our book's Discord space

Join the book's Discord Workspace for Latest updates, Offers, Tech happenings around the world, New Release and Sessions with the Authors:

https://discord.bpbonline.com

CHAPTER 10
Communication with the Views

Introduction

It has been quite a ride until now!

We are getting closer to the end of the journey. After learning about views, model, controllers, Blazor, .Net MAUI, WinUI and more, it is now time to get to know how the views can communicate between each other and with other components.

We will go back to MVC and MVVM and see the ways of communication and show same examples of them.

We will review a bit what are the views, how they are created and integrated.

Hope this point will help in understanding and learning more on .Net 7 and views.

In the following figure is a diagram remembering the difference between MVC and MVVM:

MVVM: View → View Model → Model

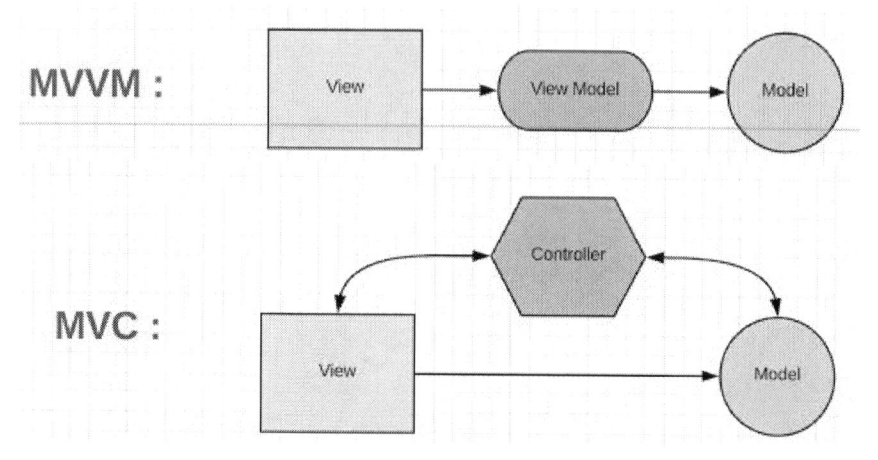

MVC: View → Controller → Model (with Controller connecting View and Model)

Figure 10.1: MVVM vs MVC

Structure

The topics that will be covered in this chapter will be:

- Ways of communication
- Examples of communication

Objectives

This chapter has the objective of learning more on how to connect and communicate between the Views and between UI and the Views.

We will go back to **Model – View - Control (MVC)** and **Model – View - View Model (MVVM)** methodologies and see how the views work and go back to previous chapter to see how UI uses and then how everything will connect.

Ways of communicating with the views

The views are the application part that handles data presentation and user interaction. Views can be designed using HTML templates with embedded Razor markup, being then saved as vbhtml or cshtml – depending on the language you are using.

As seen before there are also partial views, that are used to reduce duplication of code and to create reusable parts of a view (it can also be very useful for modals, or pop-up windows).

There is also another view type, which is view components, that is similar to partial views, because it can also simplify and reduce code duplication and repetition, but these are more appropriate to use when the content requires code to run on the server, to render the webpage.

The benefit of views

Views are good to separate concerns and information, in an MVC application, as they separate user interface from the other parts of the app.

Regarding benefits on using views, we can show some of them:

- It is easier to maintain an application due to the way they are organized. They usually are grouped by feature and by subject.

- It gets simpler to update the different parts separately. You can change a view without needing to change business layer or data access part, for example.

- The testing of the user interface parts gets easier because the views are separate units.

- It simplifies code and reduces the possibility of code repetition, due to the organization on separate layers (views, business, data, etc.)

How a controller calls a view

The controller is the programmatic part of a program that is responsible for getting the data that is required to a view template to render a response.

A view template must not contain business logic and interact directly with database. It must only work with the data that the controller passes to it. This will help the code to be more clean, testable, and maintainable.

Controllers can interact with the views and will specify them in the following way:

- Views are returned from actions as **ViewResult** (a type of **ActionResult**)
- The action method can create and return a **ViewResult**, but that cannot be done in a very easy way, so you can just directly return the View helper method – this will return a **ViewResult**.

Next, is a code sample of this call:

```
1. public IActionResult TestView()
2. {
3.
4.     return View();
5. }
```

This call will then allow the code to show the **View**, as seen in *Figure 10.2*:

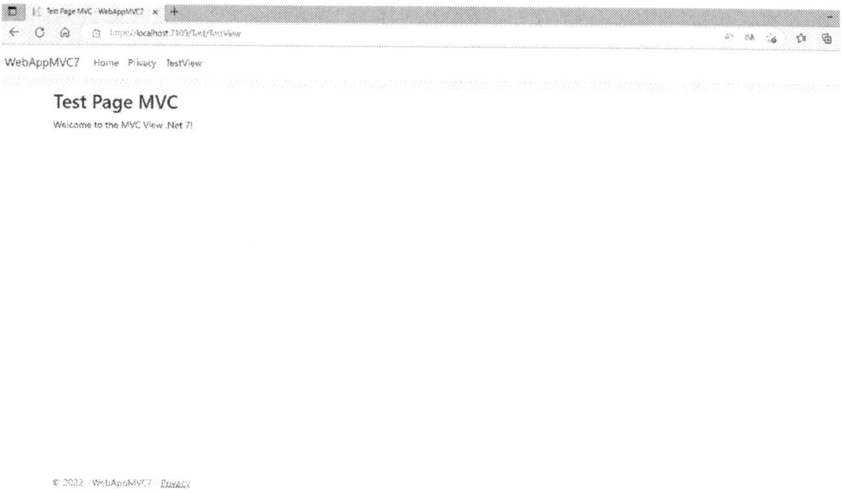

Figure 10.2: View called by the controller

The **View** helper method can be called with some overloads:

- With no parameters, as it is in the example.
- With an explicit **View** name as parameter.

```
return View("TestView");
```

- With a Model as parameter

    `return View(TestView);`

- With a **View** and a model as parameters

    `return View("TestView", TestView);`

When a view is returned from an action, it will begin a process called view discovery, which will determine what view file will be used, based on the view name.

By default, the view method will return a view with the same name as the action method that calls it. The **TestView** method name will be used to open **TestView.cshtml**. The runtime will try to find the view in the views folder. If it does not find a matching view, it will then search in the shared folder.

You can call the **View** explicitly by passing the view name to the method by using **return View("<ViewName>");** or implicitly just using **return View();**

Either way, view discovery will search for a matching view file in this order:

- **Views/ControllerName/ViewName.cshtml**
- **Views/Shared/ViewName.cshtml**

Pass data to views

Data can be passed to views, using different ways:

- Strongly typed data: **ViewModel**
- Weakly typed data
    - ViewData
    - ViewBag

Using strongly typed data is the most robust way to specify a model type in a view. It is usually referred as **ViewModel**. The instance of the **ViewModel** can be passed to the view from the action.

With **ViewModel** to pass data to a View is advantageous because of the usage of strong type checking, which means that every variable and constant has explicitly defined types (**string, int, DateTime**) with validity of type being checked at compile time.

132 ■ .NET 7 for Jobseekers

In Visual Studio, you have IntelliSense to help listing strongly typed class members. If you wish to see the properties of the **ViewModel**, you can type variable name for the **ViewModel**, followed by a period, which will help wite code faster.

In the View code (cshtml file) you can specify a model with **@Model** directive, as in the next sample taken from Microsoft learn:

```
1.  @model WebApplication1.ViewModels.Address
2.
3.  <h2>Contact</h2>
4.  <address>
5.      @Model.Street<br>
6.      @Model.City, @Model.State @Model.PostalCode<br>
7.      <abbr title="Phone">P:</abbr> 425.555.0100
8.  </address>
```

The model will be passed as a parameter, to the view, by the controller:

```
1.  public IActionResult Contact()
2.  {
3.      ViewData["Message"] = "Your contact page.";
4.
5.      var viewModel = new Address()
6.      {
7.          Name = "Microsoft",
8.          Street = "One Microsoft Way",
9.          City = "Redmond",
10.         State = "WA",
11.         PostalCode = "98052-6399"
12.     };
13.
14.     return View(viewModel);
15. }
```

You can save the **ViewModel** classes in the **Models** folder or separate **ViewModels** folder, at the application root.

It is also recommended the usage of separate models allowing the views to vary independently from the business logic and data access parts of the application.

Another way to pass data to the **View** is using weakly typed data, such as **ViewData, [ViewData]** attribute and **ViewBag**.

These can be used to pass data between:

- Controller and View
- View and Layout View
- Partial View and View

The **ViewData** is a dictionary of weakly typed objects; the **ViewBag** is a wrapper around **ViewData**, which will provide dynamic properties for its collection. They both are dynamically resolved at runtime, and because they do not have compile-time type checking, they are more possible to generate errors than the **ViewModel**.

Now let us see how each of these typed data works, starting by **ViewData**:

- It is an object, of **ViewDataDictionary** type that can be accessed using string keys. When extracting data other than String, it must be used a cast to the object specific type. This type can be used to pass data from controller to views and between views, and partial views and layouts.

- Next, is an example, from Microsoft learn, of a value setting using **ViewData** in an action. First, is the code behind C# code:

```
1. public IActionResult SomeAction()
2. {
3.    ViewData["Greeting"] = "Hello";
4.    ViewData["Address"]  = new Address()
5.    {
6.       Name = "Steve",
7.       Street = "123 Main St",
8.       City = "Hudson",
9.       State = "OH",
10.      PostalCode = "44236"
```

```
11. };
12. return View();
13. }
```

And now, the cshtml:

```
1. @{
2.     // Since Address is not a string, it requires a cast.
3.     var address = ViewData["Address"] as Address;
4. }
5.
6. @ViewData["Greeting"] World!
7.
8. <address>
9.     @address.Name<br>
10.    @address.Street<br>
11.    @address.City, @address.State @address.PostalCode
12. </address>
```

Now, another approach we can see is [**ViewData**] attribute:

- It is an attribute, of **ViewDataAttribute** type that uses the **ViewDataDictionary**. When a property on controllers or Razor Page models are marked with this attribute, the correspondent values are stored and loaded from the dictionary.

- Next, is an example from Microsoft learn, of a property with the [**ViewData**] attribute and the value setting on that property. First, from the C# side:

```
1. public class HomeController : Controller
2. {
3.     [ViewData]
4.     public string Title { get; set; }
5.
6.     public IActionResult About()
7.     {
```

8.   Title = "About Us";
9.   ViewData["Message"] = "Your application description page.";
10.
11.   return View();
12.   }
13. }

And the cshtml:

1. <!DOCTYPE html>
2. <html lang="en">
3. <head>
4.   <title>@ViewData["Title"] - WebApplication</title>
5.   ...

Another approach we can use is **ViewBag**:

- This approach is not available by default for use in Razor Pages **PageModel** classes.
- This is a **Microsoft.AspNetCore.Mvc.ViewFeatures. Internal.DynamicViewData** object that gives dynamic access to the objects that are in **ViewData**.
- It is easier and simpler to use, due to the fact it does not need require casting.
- Next, is shown as an example, also from Microsoft Learn, using a **ViewBag** with the same result as the one seen in **ViewData**. First, the C# code:

1. public IActionResult SomeAction()
2. {
3.   ViewBag.Greeting = "Hello";
4.   ViewBag.Address = new Address()
5.   {
6.   Name = "Steve",
7.   Street = "123 Main St",
8.   City = "Hudson",
9.   State = "OH",

```
10.         PostalCode = "44236"
11.     };
12.
13.     return View();
14. }
```

Now, for the cshtml code:

```
1. @ViewBag.Greeting World!
2.
3. <address>
4.     @ViewBag.Address.Name<br>
5.     @ViewBag.Address.Street<br>
6.     @ViewBag.Address.City, @ViewBag.Address.State @ViewBag.Address.PostalCode
7. </address>
```

Also, we can use **ViewData** and **ViewBag** simultaneously, as they refer to the same **ViewData** collection. We can even mix and match between both when reading and writing.

In this next Microsoft learn example, we can see this mix and match on the cshtml page:

```
1. @{
2.     Layout = "/Views/Shared/_Layout.cshtml";
3.     ViewBag.Title = "About Contoso";
4.     ViewData["Description"] = "Let us tell you about Contoso's philosophy and mission.";
5. }
```

Model-View-Controller

Model-View-Controller (MVC) is one of the most used architectures, in development, and of course, it will also be in .Net 7.

In the following figure there is an example of the MVC architecture:

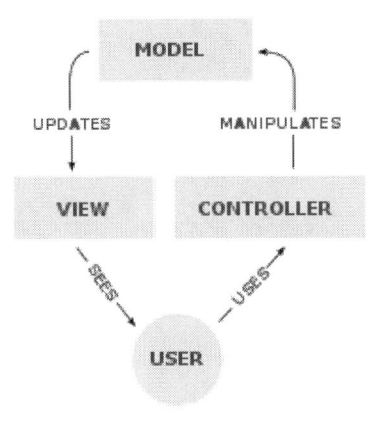

Figure 10.3: MVC architecture

In MVC, the communication to the views can be done in 3 ways: Model to View, View to View and Controller to View.

Let us see these communication methods, starting with Model to View:

- The path to this way of communication is Model | Controller | View

- The Model is made in the Controller, then it is passed to the View.

- The data can be passed from Model to View by doing the following:

    o In the Controller, take the object in its action.

    o Pass the object as a parameter from the Model to the View.

    o Use the tagline @model to include the Model in the View.

Another way to communicate, is View to View, which is simpler and only work using partial Views to move from one View to another.

Partial Views can access data from model, by receiving it in one of the following ways:

- Using `ViewDataDictionary`

1. `@await Html.PartialAsync("_PartialName", customViewData)`

- Using the model directly

1. `@await Html.PartialAsync("_PartialName", model)`

Finally, Controller to View can be done in these ways:

- Using ViewBag
- With ViewData
- Or, With TempData

There is also the possibility of the reverse communication: View to Model and View to Controller.

View to Model communication can be done using the path View | Controller | Model. The data must be passed to the Controller which will then send it to the Model. The steps that must be followed to pass data to the Model are:

1. Submit an HTML from to a Controller.
2. Create a Model object in the Controller.
3. Pass the values to the Model.

When communicating from View to Controller, the form must be submitted from View to Controller directly or using JSON, AJAX Calls, Javascript or Pratial Views.

Model-View-ViewModel (MVVM)

As seen before, this interactions between Views and other components can be made in the already seen **MVC** but also in MVVM.

But what is MVVM? It is an architectural pattern to simplify the separation of the graphic interface and the business logic.

We have a model, which is an object that can be a domain model or data access layer. also, there is a view, which represents the structure, layout, and appearance of what is seen by the user. it will show a representation of the model and will receive a user interaction, passing the handling of these interactions to the ViewModel, though data binding, which will link between View and ViewModel.

Finally, it will have a ViewModel, which is an abstraction of the View. The ViewModel will also have a binder, that will automate the communication between View and the properties in the ViewModel. A View will directly bind the properties on the ViewModel to send and receive updates.

This Binder, in MVVM is a markup language called **Extensible Application Markup Language (XAML)**

Figure 10.4 illusrates the architecture of MVVM.

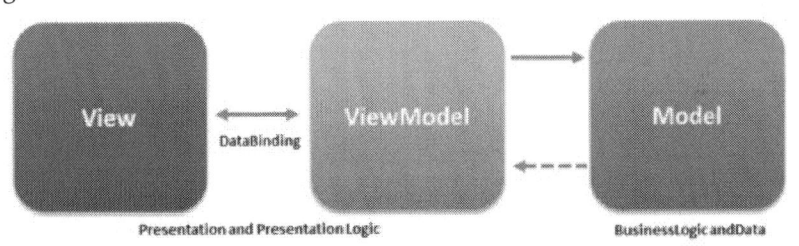

Figure 10.4: MVVM architecture

Conclusion

In this chapter we have learned a bit more about Views and how they communicate.

We have been navigating through the waves of MVC, getting to know Models, Views and Controllers, and how they interact. Also, we have travelled to Blazor, .Net MAUI and WinUI.

But, in this chapter we gave a step back and returned to the Views, learning more about them and the way they communicate between each other and with other components.

Also, we have learned a bit about not only the MVC, but the MVVM, which is a different approach on development.

We hope this has been an interesting and fructuous chapter, with useful thoughts and new learning points.

Next, we will have a chapter on another recent feature: SignalR.

So, prepare yourselves for what is coming, as we're approaching the end of our journey.

Join our book's Discord space

Join the book's Discord Workspace for Latest updates, Offers, Tech happenings around the world, New Release and Sessions with the Authors:

https://discord.bpbonline.com

Chapter 11
Use SignalR

Introduction

Well, we are on the way to the end our journey.

But first, we will now travel to the world of SignalR.

After all that we have been learning, it is now time to learn what is SignalR. We will go through several points, starting with the definition of the framework, passing by the improvements that .Net 7 brings to it, how this can be used and what can be done using ASP. Net and SignalR.

Finally, we will go through the advantages of SignalR and what it can be bring to development.

This is a great framework, and we hope you will enjoy and learn a lot, having fun through the next pages!

To get started, we leave you **SignalR** logo from .Net, in the following figure:

Figure 11.1: SignalR Logo

Structure

The topics that will be covered in this chapter will be:

- What is SignalR and how to use it
- Advantages of SignalR
- What can you do with ASP.Net and SignalR
- Improvements in .Net 7

Objectives

This chapter has the objective of learning more on SignalR.

We will go through What is SignalR, what does it brings new in .Net 7, how to use it and what can be done with it in ASP.Net.

Also, we will get to know the advantages of SignalR.

What is SignalR and how to use it

Let us start travelling through SignalR, but first is important to learn what the reality is.

SignalR is an ASP.Net library that helps developers to add real-time functionalities into web applications. It will allow web functionalities to send content to all end-users, instead of just getting the server to wait for the client requests.

One good example of an application that can be done using SignalR is a chat application.

Today, it is very important that applications can send information to all users without having to refresh the web page – for example, notifications and newsfeeds. So, we will need a real-time server connection to get the data, which can be done using SignalR.

Following, is a schema of a web API that uses SignalR to send messages to all users:

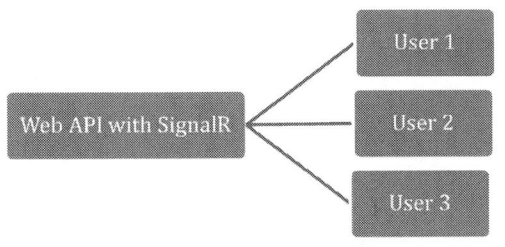

Figure 11.2: *SignalR Schema Sample*

In the schema of *Figure 11.2*, we can see one server sending messages to three users. An example of a website where this will happen can be an eCommerce site where the admin can send, for example, product offers to all the subscribers, and all the users will receive the offer details. For this, SignalR is very important, because it will allow the information to be delivered easily and in real time to all the users at the same time.

But what are the real benefits of using SignalR? Let us check it out in the next points:

- SignalR allows bi-directional communication between one server and many clients at a time.
- It will allow to broadcast messages to one or several clients.
- When we need to send notifications, feed updates, alert messages, or some product offers, SignalR is easy and efficient.
- It can easily create a real-time chat application to be used by several users at the same time, providing great user experience.

Regardless, SignalR **cannot** be seen as a replacement for traditional HTTP requests, but as a complement to it.

How SignalR works in ASP.Net Core applications

SignalR, in ASP.Net Core uses the **Hub** Class, that is defined in `Microsoft.AspNetCore.SignalR` namespace. If an app already uses `Microsoft.Net.Sdk.Web`, this package already contains SignalR as a shared framework.

The Hub is represented and called using a route. With the several hub APIs, the programmers can define methods and events.

We can expose methods on a hub, using a subclass of these two types and write methods:

- **Hub**: A standard hub
- **Hub <T>**: A strongly typed generic hub

The events can be fired from a Hub or `IHubContext`. This hub is a core abstraction that sends messages to clients connected to a SignalR server.

To send messages from other sides on the app, you can use one of these types:

- **IHubContext<THub>**: In this context, **THub** is a standard hub
- **IHubContext<THub,T>**: In this context, **THub** is a strongly typed generic hub, and T is the corresponding type of client.

Hub methods are used like other C# method. They have a return type, which most commonly can be a `Task` or `Task<TResult>` that will represent an asynchronous hub operation. They will have optional parameters that, when defined, must be provided with the corresponding arguments.

The server can also raise events, which will be named and can define up to ten parameters. They will be fired on server side and will be handled by clients.

The HubConnection class

This class is a SignalR client concept that will represent client's connection to the Hub server and it is defined in `Microsoft.AspNetCore.SignalR.Client` namespace.

Next, is an example, taken from Microsoft Learn, on how to create this `HubConnection` object, using .Net SignalR client SDK:

```
1. using Microsoft.AspNetCore.SignalR.Client;
2. using System;
3. using System.Threading.Tasks;
```

```
4. using RealTime.Models;
5.
6. namespace ExampleClient;
7.
8. public sealed class Consumer : IAsyncDisposable
9. {
10.    private readonly string HostDomain =
11.           Environment.GetEnvironmentVariable("HOST_DOMAIN");
12.
13.    private HubConnection _hubConnection;
14.
15.    public Consumer()
16.    {
17.        _hubConnection = new HubConnectionBuilder()
18.            .WithUrl(new Uri($"{HostDomain}/hub/notifications"))
19.            .WithAutomaticReconnect()
20.            .Build();
21.    }
22.
23.    public Task StartNotificationConnectionAsync() =>
24.        _hubConnection.StartAsync();
25.
26.    public async ValueTask DisposeAsync()
27.    {
28.        if (_hubConnection is not null)
29.        {
30.            await _hubConnection.DisposeAsync();
31.            _hubConnection = null;
32.        }
33.    }
34. }
```

After having the `HubConnection`, the client can then call hub methods, using `InvokeAsync` or `SendAsync`. When the method returns `Task<TResult>`, the result of the `InvokeAsync<TResult>` will be of type `TResult`. When the return type of the method, is `Task`, there's no result.

Both methods `InvokeAsync` and `SendAsync` will invoke the hub method on the server, using its name and optional arguments, but `SendAsync` will not wait for a response.

Advantages of SignalR

SignalR will use WebSockets as the underlying transport, but will have additional features:

- It will allow reconnections to be made automatically.
- It is an alternative to other transports.
- It will have an API to create server to client remote procedure calls.
- It will allow to send a message to all clients that are connected, at once.

The advantages of using SignalR are:

- Several options that can be used to scaling out: Redis, SQL Server, Azure Service Bus.
- It is part of .Net Framework, which makes it easy to use, combined with other ASP.Net features, such as authentication, authorization, and dependency injection.
- It will use WebSockets, but also supports Server Sent Events and HTTP long pooling.

WebSockets is a technique built in the browser, notifying the server when the browser sends something to it. This process establishes full-duplex communication using TCP protocol, for the two-way process between client-server.

Long pooling is a new technique, that uses HTTP protocol to send data from the server to the client, holding the connection open as much time as possible and only sending data when needed.

But, of course, using SignalR will also have its challenges. Let's look at them:

- It has a weak messaging quality of service because it is not guaranteed the ordering and delivery. You must develop a mechanism that will ensure this.

- It has a limited number of client SDKs, by only being available in C#, Java, Python and Javascript.

- There is no SDK available for mobile platforms, such as iOS or Android.

- It's designed to be used in a single region and this will have impact on performance, availability, and reliability.

- It is difficult, expensive, and time-consuming to scale SignalR. To not having to do that, you can use Azure SignalR service, but it will have its own limitations, such as a maximum 99.95% uptime guarantee.

What can you do with ASP.Net and SignalR

It is now time to learn a bit on how to use ASP.Net Core together with SignalR.

So, lets follow these steps and try to create a chat.

First, we will have to create a web project, as seen in the following figure:

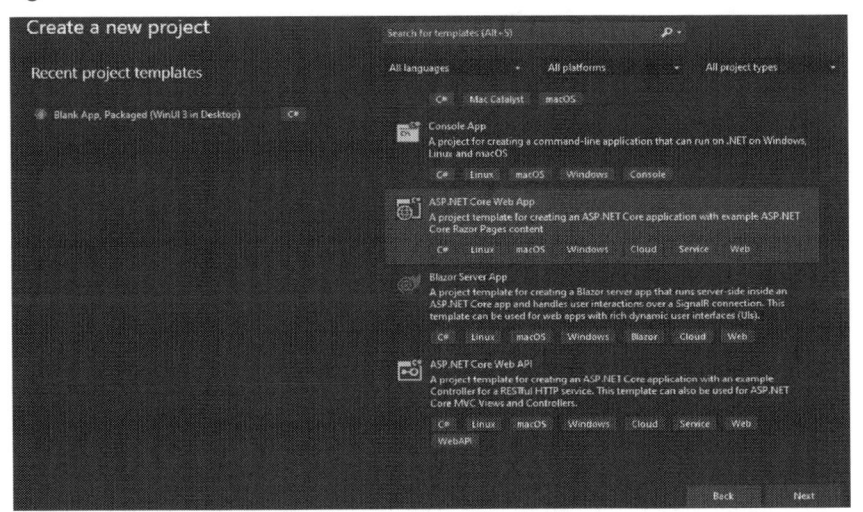

Figure 11.3: Create an ASP.Net Core Web App

148 ■ .NET 7 for Jobseekers

Next, name your project as shown in *Figure 11.4*:

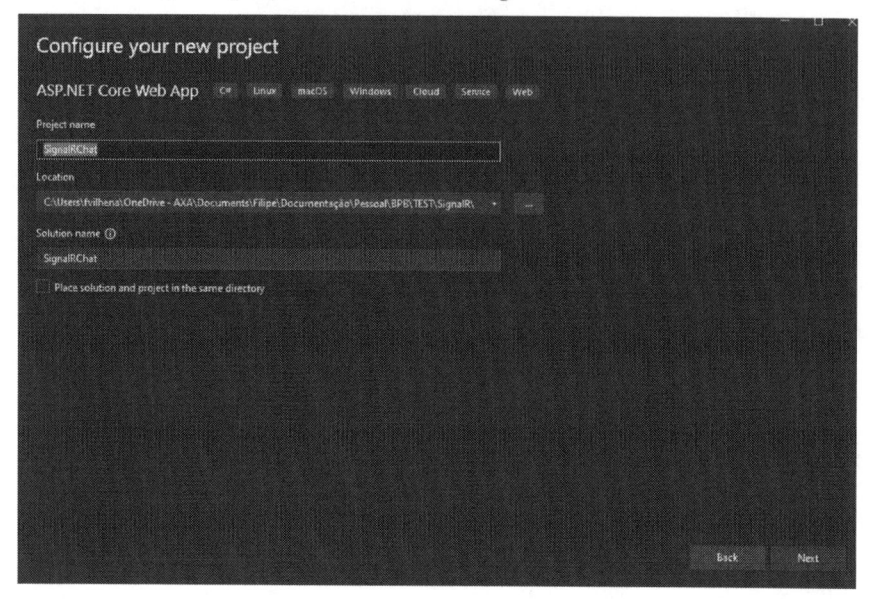

Figure 11.4: Rename your application

Now, it is time to select the **Framework**, and we will choose **.Net 7**, like it is in the following figure:

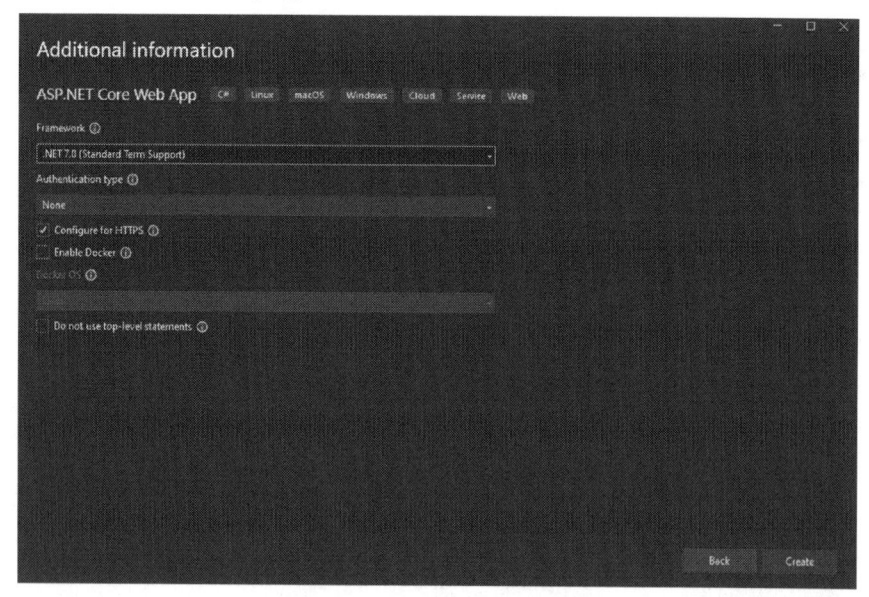

Figure 11.5: Select Framework

Use SignalR ■ 149

To use SignalR, we need to add it in the project as it isn't automatically included in the project.

To add it, we need to follow these steps:

1. In your project, in Visual Studio, go to **Solution Explorer**, right-click the project and select **Add | Client-Side Library**.

2. In the dialog that shows, fill it as shown in the following figure:

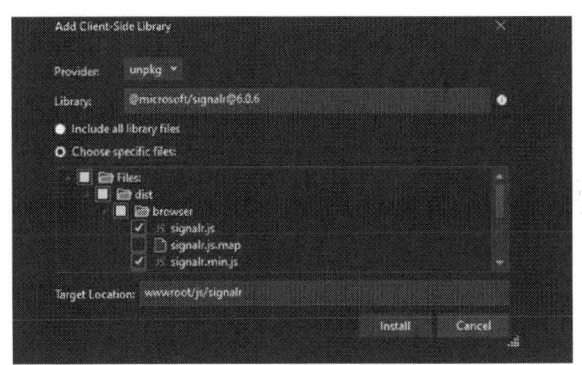

Figure 11.6: Add Client-Side Library

Next, we will have to create the SignalR hub, by doing the following:

1. Go to the **Project** folder and create a **Hubs** folder.

2. In this folder, add a Class, which you can call **ChatHub**, with the code as it is in *Figure 11.7*:

Figure 11.7: Add ChatHub class

This class will inherit from SignalR default **Hub** class, which will manage connections, groups, and messages.

The method used (**SendMessage**) can be called by the clients that are connected, for message sending to all clients. SignalR has asynchronous code, so it will have more scalability.

By adding an interface, we can also add a strong type method "**Receive Message**" to be used in the code above.

To continue, we must add to **Program.cs**, the following code, to configure SignalR server:

- You must add this *using*:

    1. using SignalRChat.Hubs;

- In the builder section, add the following line:

    1. builder.Services.AddSignalR();

- This next line can be added at the end, before **app.Run();**

    1. app.MapHub<ChatHub>("/chatHub");

After having this done, we must change the code of **Index.cshtml** to the one shown in the *Figure 11.8*:

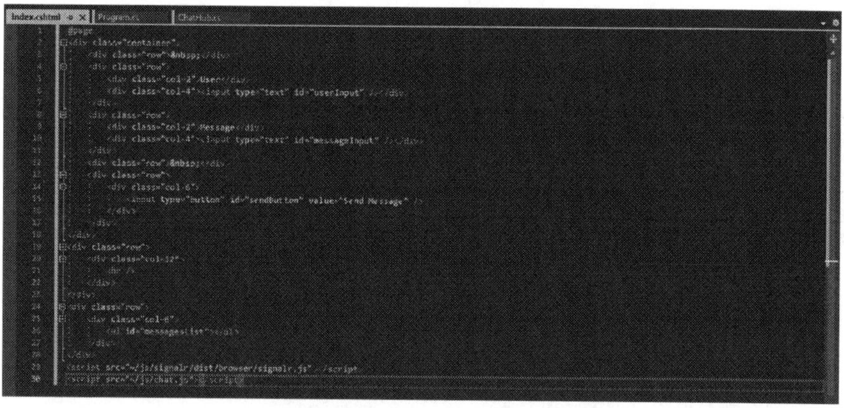

Figure 11.8: Index.cshtml code

This will create text boxes and a submit button, and a list for displaying messages received from SignalR hub. It will also have a reference to the **chat.js** Javascript file, which must be created in **wwwroot/js** folder, and have the code seen in the following figure:

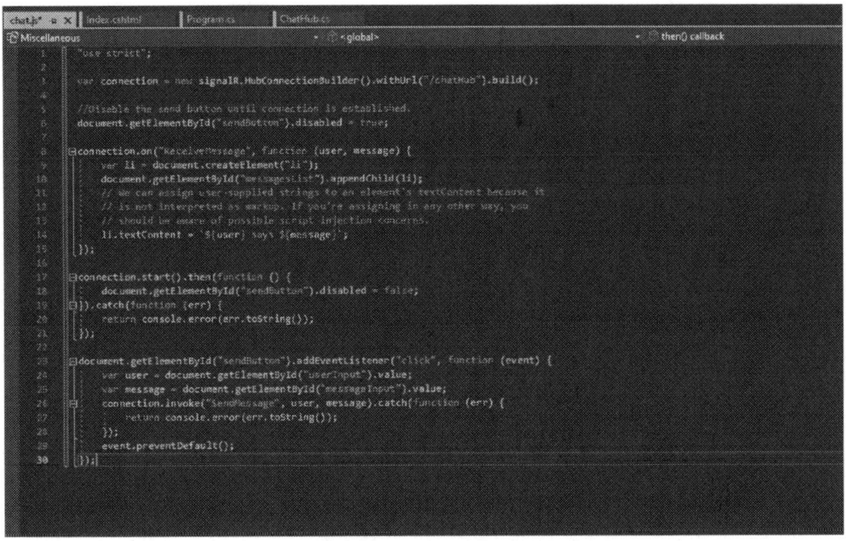

Figure 11.9: chat.js file

This JavaScript file will create and start a connection and will add the handler to that button, so that it will send messages to the hub. Also, it adds the handler that receives messages from the hub and will add them to the list.

Now, everything is done and configured, so you just need to run your application by pressing *CTRL+F5*.

This will open a Chat page. You must copy the url to another browser instance and send messages in each other.

You will then get something like it is shown in *Figure 11.10*:

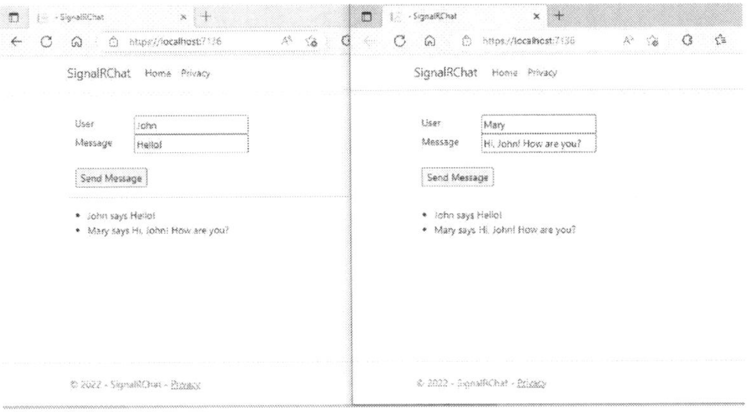

Figure 11.10: SignalR Chat sample

Improvements in .Net 7

.Net 7 will bring some improvements to SignalR, so it can be easily used. Now, let's go through some of them:

- Before .Net 7, it was necessary to apply **[FromService]** attribute to a parameter, so it is defined as service sourced. Now, we can use parameter binding for API controller actions, which will allow to bind them using dependency injections, as we can see in this example from Microsoft:

```
1. Services.AddScoped<SomeCustomType>();
2.
3. [Route("[controller]")]
4. [ApiController]
5. public class MyController : ControllerBase
6. {
7.     // Both actions will bound the SomeCustomType from the DI container
8.     public ActionResult GetWithAttribute([FromServices]SomeCustomType service) => Ok();
9.     public ActionResult Get(SomeCustomType service) => Ok();
10. }
```

- Besides linking the parameters, using injection, it is also possible to disable it if we don't want to use it. It's just needed to use **DisableImplicitFromServicesParameters**, as we can see in the following Microsoft example:

```
1. Services.Configure<ApiBehaviorOptions>(options =>
2. {
3.     options.DisableImplicitFromServicesParameters = true;
4. })
```

- In .Net 7, it was also added a client source generator for SignalR but now, with dependency injection, we are able to inject services with SignalR hub methods, as it is shown in the following example, from Microsoft:

Use SignalR ■ 153

```
1. Services.AddScoped<SomeCustomType>();
2.
3. public class MyHub : Hub
4. {
5.     // SomeCustomType comes from DI by default now
6.     public Task Method(string text, SomeCustomType type) => Task.CompletedTask;
7. }
```

- Also, it is possible to mark only one parameter, in an explicit way, which can be useful when we want to link only that parameter from the configured services. It can be done using the **[FromServices]** attribute, as seen in the next example, also taken from Microsoft:

```
1. public class MyHub : Hub
2. {
3.     public Task Method(string arguments, [FromServices] SomeCustomType type);
4. }
```

- The Dependency Injection can also be disabled, configuring **DisableImplicitFromServicesParameters**, as seen in the next Microsoft example:

```
1. services.AddSignalR(options =>
2. {
3.     options.DisableImplicitFromServicesParameters = true;
4. });
```

- We can also, in .Net 7 set summaries and descriptions for route handlers, when using minimal APIs. We can see a Microsoft example of how it is done:

```
1. app.MapGet("/hello", () => ...)
2.   .WithDescription("Sends a request to the back-end HelloService to process a greeting request.");
```

- It is possible to set summary or description, by using an attribute on the route handler delegate, as seen in the following code sample:

1. `app.MapGet("/hello", [EndpointSummary("Sends a Hello request to the backend")]() => ...)`

- Another feature added in .Net 7 is the possibility to bind query strings and HTTPS header values to **StringValues** or any primitive type array.

- There is now also the possibility to add a custom value for tracking cookies, using **CookiePolicyOptions. ConsentCookieValue**.

Conclusion

We are arriving at the end of our journey.

In this chapter we have learned about SignalR, starting by what it really is and going a bit through some of its points, and how it can be used.

Also, we have seen some of SignalR advantages and challenges.

We went through some information and examples of what can be done using ASP.Net and SignalR.

Finally, we have discovered the news that .Net 7 brings to SignalR.

We hope this was a great step in our journey and that you have loved it and been able to learn new things and discover the world of SignalR.

In the next chapter, we will learn about databases and how to add and use them in .Net 7.

Now relax and get ready for the final steps of our journey.

Join our book's Discord space

Join the book's Discord Workspace for Latest updates, Offers, Tech happenings around the world, New Release and Sessions with the Authors:

https://discord.bpbonline.com

Chapter 12
Adding a Database

Introduction

Another chapter in our journey is now starting.

We will learn about databases and how to add them to a project in .Net 7.

We will go through the basics and see how we can add a database and how to integrate databases using MVC, in .Net 7.

Databases can be very useful several operations and have always been integrated in .Net, especially SQL Server and Entity Framework, so this will not be different in .Net 7.

So, in the following pages we will learn a bit about how they work and how to integrate it in this framework version of .Net.

In *Figure 12.1* is a representation of how ADO.Net (ActiveX Data Objects) works with Databases in .Net framework:

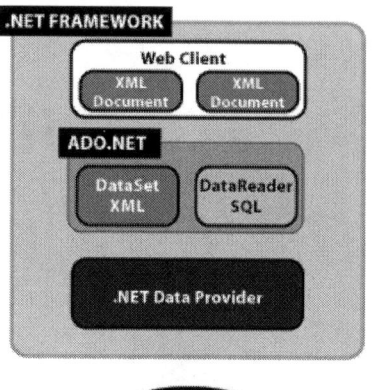

Figure 12.1: *Databases in .Net*

Structure

The following topics that will be covered in this chapter will be:

- Add the database
- Ways of using databases
- Entity framework 7
- Ways of integration of databases using MVC and .Net 7

Objectives

This chapter has the objective getting to know a bit more about databases.

We will go through how to add the database and use it .Net 7, seeing ways of integration databases, using MVC.

Adding the database

In every .Net project, being .Net 7 or previous, it is important to use databases. They will help you to store your data and allow to perform **Create, Read, Update, Delete (CRUD)** operations on it.

You can use a lot of database types but the more used in .Net projects are:

- **SQL Server**: Since this is Microsoft proprietary, and it is the first one that Entity Framework is developed for, it is the more recommended and used in .Net projects. It is also possible to use SQL Server Developer Edition for free, so it will help the usage of this database type.
- **MySQL**: It has been acquired by Oracle in 2010, but remains open source, which is a plus for increasing its usage.
- **PostgreSQL**: This is quite popular and is gaining lots of fans, due to the fact of being also open source and with a permissive license.

Below is a figure containing the logos for these three databases:

Figure 12.2: *Most used Databases in .Net*

It is possible to add a database, using Visual Studio – for example, with Transact-SQL statements in SQL Server Object -, or directly in SQL Server Management Studio (for SQL, of course).

To create a project with a local database we can follow these steps:

1. Create a Windows Form App (for example), save it in your preferred folder and give it a name.

158 ■ .NET 7 for Jobseekers

2. In *Figure 12.3*, on the menu bar, select **Project | Add New item** and select **Service-based Database**, as seen in the following figure:

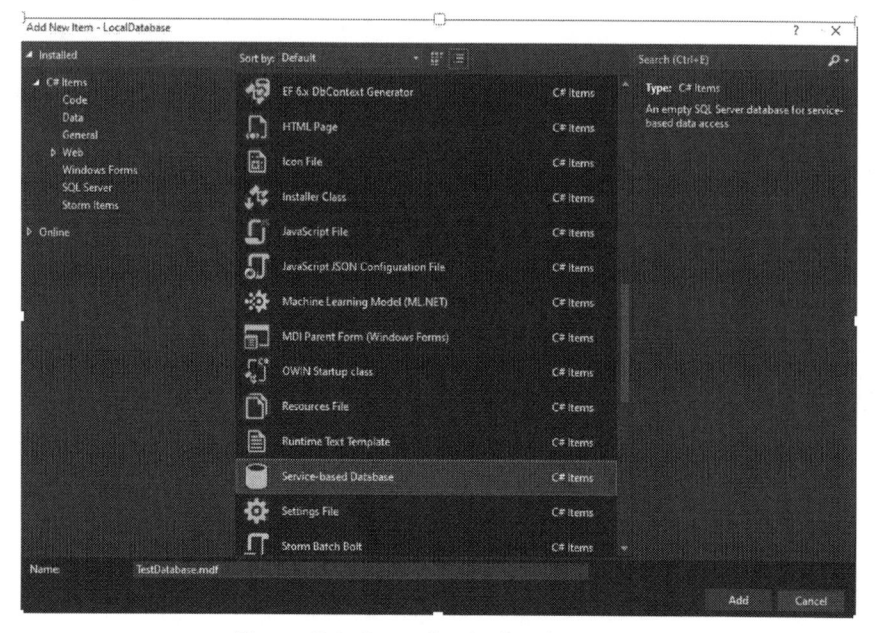

Figure 12.3: Create Service-based Database

3. Open Data Sources Window and select **Add New Data Source**, as following:

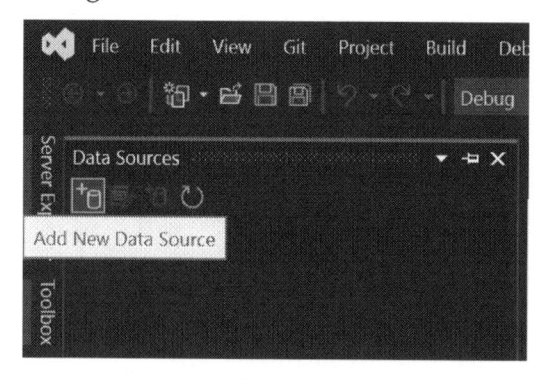

Figure 12.4: Add New Data Source

4. It will open Data Source Configuration Wizard, where you need to choose **Database**, on **Choose Data Source Type**. Next accept the default, on **Choose a Database Model** and select your .mdf database file on the **Choose your data connection** page.

5. Save the Connection String to the Application Configuration File and then **Finish** the Wizard.

6. Then, we can create some tables, on **Server Explorer**, by right-clicking **Tables** | **Add New Table**, as seen in the following figure:

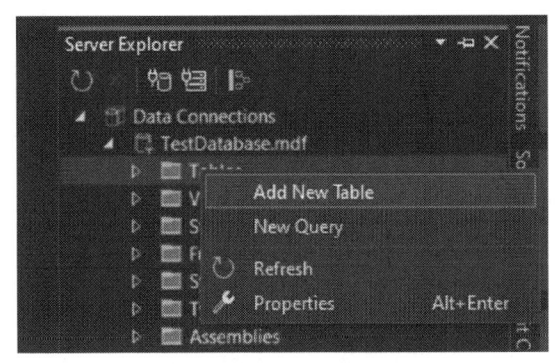

Figure 12.5: Add New Table

7. Now, it is possible to add the fields you want and name the Table what you prefer. You can see in *Figure 12.6*, an example of how to fill it. Also, you can define a primary Key.

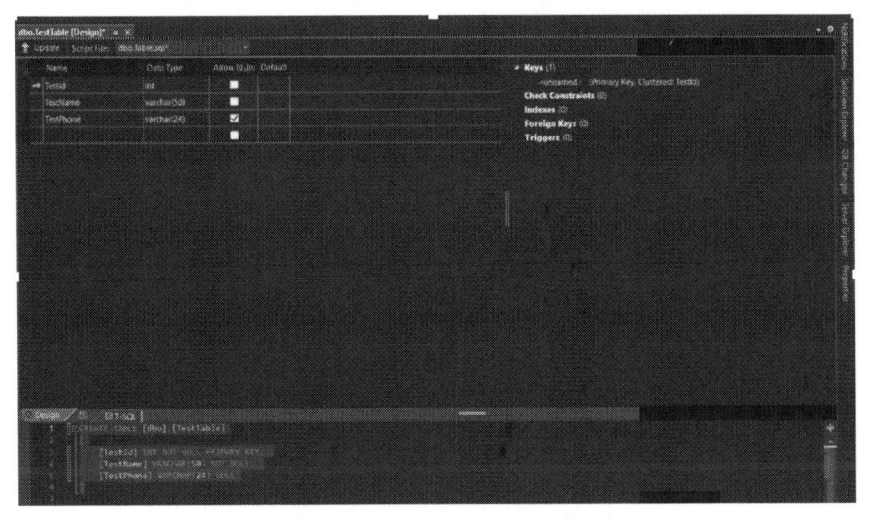

Figure 12.6: Create Table and add Table Fields

8. When you are done, go to the upper-left corner of **Table Designer** and select **Update**. On the dialog box, seen in the

following figure, select **Update Database**, and this will create the table in your local database.

Figure 12.7: Update Database to create the table

9. After this, you can add more tables, and populate them with data that can then be used in your application.

Ways of using databases

Besides the example seen in previous point, we can use databases in several other ways.

For more secure usage, you can, for example, integrate the database connections into Azure and into the **appsettings.json** file.

This approach can also turn database access faster and it can simplify the usage of databases.

Following are the multiple ways we commonly use databases is:

- On my MVC or Razor project, we store database connection into the **appsettings.json** file.
- We use **Program.cs** or **Startup.cs** to define scopes, authentication, and authorizations.
- Then we use Model files to define the properties that will be Serialized with the database fields – one file per table.

- Then we integrate these Data Models with Domain Models and connect all of them using App files which we call Service files, and that will contain the methods needed for reading, adding, updating, and deleting data.
- If needed and depending on the needs, we can also use some View Models in a **Model-View-View Model (MVVM)** approach.

The following figure is a diagram representation of my usual approach:

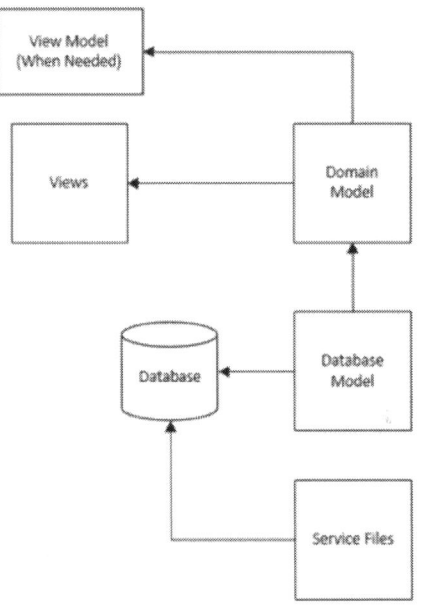

Figure 12.8: Diagram of database usage

Entity framework 7

Another way to access and use databases is with **Entity Framework (EF)**. EF is part of .Net Framework and is used to map ADO.Net objects. In the following figure is EF Core logo:

Figure 12.9: Entity Framework Core logo

As other things, it has new improvements in .Net 7. We will now go through some of them to explain how to connect and use databases.

SqlClient strings now use by default Encrypt = true which means that the server now must configured with a valid certificate, on which the client must trust.

If that is not accomplished you will have an SQLException with the following message: *provider: SSL Provider, error: 0 – The certificate chain was issued by an authority that is not trusted.*

This is a change that was made by security reasons to guarantee that your application will always have secure connections, or else it will fail.

Two new methods are now introduced: **ExecuteUpdate** and **ExecuteDelete**. These methods will be applied to a LINQ query and will update or delete database entities. You can update many different entities with a single command and these entities will not be stored in memory, making the query and process more efficient.

Following is a sample of the usage of **ExecuteDelete**, which will delete all the elements that correspond to the filter.

```
1.  var excludedData = context.SampleTable
2.          .Where(p => p.Name.Contains("Test"))
3.          .ExecuteDelete();
```

This command will allow deleting all elements from our **SampleTable** that will have the word "**Test**" on its Name. It will generate a simple Query to Delete data from our database, as shown following:

```
1.  DELETE FROM [ST]
2.  FROM [SAMPLETABLE] AS [ST]
3.  WHERE [ST].[NAME] LIKE N'%TEST%'
```

Now let us look at some examples of how **ExecuteUpdate** and **ExecuteUpdateAsync** work. They are very similar to **ExecuteDelete**, being the main difference the fact that we need to know what properties we have to update and how.

To do that, we must call the method **SetProperty** with the following syntax, seen in this following example:

```
1.  await context.SampleTable.ExecuteUpdateAsync(
2.      s => s.SetProperty(b => b.Name, b => b.
    Name+ " *Updated!*"));
```

The first argument will select the property to be update and the second arguments will represent the new value of the property.

In the example used for **ExecuteDelete**, we will now update the property Name, also using a condition to update several rows.

Let us see how it will be in this code sample:

```
1. var updatedData = context.SampleTable
2.    .Where(p => p.TableId<= 80)
3.    .ExecuteUpdate(p => p.SetProperty(x => x.
   Name, x => "FullyUpdated"));
```

If you want to update more than one property at once, you'll have to invoke **SetProperty** method more than once, as seen in the following example:

```
1. var updatedData = context.SampleTable.Where(p => p.
   TableId<= 80)
2.         .ExecuteUpdate(p => p.SetProperty(n => n.
   Name, n => "New Name")
3.                       .SetProperty(e => e.
   Email, e => "New Email"));
```

Be aware as these methods will only be able to work in one table, so carefully prepare your work, before organizing the mappings and the executions.

New interceptors and events in EF

Entity Framework also brings some news in interceptors and events, for .Net 7.

So, interceptors, which enable intercept, modify, and supress EF Core operations, now have the following improvements and functionalities:

- Creating and populating new entity instances
- Modify LINQ expression tree before a query is compiled
- Optimistic concurrency handling
- Before checking if exists a connection string, it will be able to have interception
- After EF Core consumes a result set, but before it is closed, it is possible to have interception

- Creating a DbConnection by EF Core
- DbCommand after initialization

Regarding events, there will be new traditional .Net events for:

- The moment before an entity is about to be tracked or having its state changed, but it isn't already tracked or had its state changed
- Before and after having been detected changes to entities and properties

JSON columns

EF Core 7 will also have some improvements regarding JSON.

Most of the relational databases have support for columns with JSON documents, and these JSON can be read and worked with queries. With this, it is possible to filter and sort by properties, inside these documents, and project the properties from the documents into results. Also, JSON columns allow relational databases to get some of the characteristics of document databases and they can be used to reduce or eliminate the joins needed in queries, with this improving performance.

In .Net 7, we will now have provider-agnostic support for these JSON columns, being then able to implement in SQL Server. This will allow mapping from .Net types to JSON documents. LINQ queries will then have the possibility to be used on aggregates, which will be passed to the query constructs needed to dive into JSON.

So, we are now able to use LINQ to make a JSON query, as seen in the following code sample from Microsoft devblogs:

```
1.   var postsWithViews = await context.Posts.
     Where(post => post.Metadata!.Views > 3000)
2.       .AsNoTracking()
3.       .Select(
4.           post => new
5.           {
6.               post.Author!.Name,
7.               post.Metadata!.Views,
8.               Searches = post.Metadata.TopSearches,
9.               Commits = post.Metadata.Updates
10.          })
11.      .ToListAsync();
```

This code will now be translated to SQL, by Entity Framework 7, into the following query:

```
1. SELECT [a].[Name],
2.          CAST(JSON_VALUE([p].[Metadata],'$.Views') AS int),
3.          JSON_QUERY([p].[Metadata],'$.TopSearches'),
4.          [p].[Id],
5.          JSON_QUERY([p].[Metadata],'$.Updates')
6. FROM [Posts] AS [p]
7. LEFT JOIN [Authors] AS [a] ON [p].[AuthorId] = [a].[Id]
8. WHERE CAST(JSON_VALUE([p].[Metadata],'$.Views') AS int) > 3000
```

Then, we can use **SaveChanges** to update JSON. Entity Framework 7 will find the smallest part of the JSON document that needs to be updated and will create a more efficient update SQL command.

Let us see how it works, following the example from Microsoft DevBlogs:

```
1. var arthur = await context.Authors.
   SingleAsync(author => author.Name.StartsWith("Arthur"));
2.
3. arthur.Contact.Address.Country = "United Kingdom";
4.
5. await context.SaveChangesAsync();
```

This will generate the following SQL parameter for the changed value:

```
1. @p0='["United King-
   dom"]' (Nullable = false) (Size = 18)
```

Then, it will use the parameter with the command **JSON_MODIFY**, as seen following:

```
1. UPDATE [Authors]
2. SET [Contact] = JSON_MODIFY([Contact], 'strict $.Address.Country', JSON_VALUE(@p0, '$[0]'))
3. OUTPUT 1
4. WHERE [Id] = @p1;
```

Custom database first templates

Entity Framework 7 supports templates that will be used for customizing scaffolded code in the cases that and EF Model was reverse engineered from the database. To add the default templates to your project, you must use this dotnet command:

1. `dotnet new --install Microsoft.EntityFrameworkCore.Templates`
2. `dotnet new ef-templates`

Then, the templates can be customized and automatically be used by `dotnet ef dbcontext scaffold` and `Scaffold-DbContext`.

Conclusion

In this chapter we have learned about databases, and how we can use them and add them to a .Net application, also using .Net 7.

We have seen what the most used databases are and how we can integrate them in an application.

We shared some examples and integrated databases in .Net 7 application and went on to see some of the changes that Entity Framework 7 now brings us.

We hope that this could have been useful and interesting, now that we are approaching the end of our journey.

But we still have a few more steps to go. In the following chapter, we will learn about Orleans and how to use it in .Net 7.

Now it is time to sit back and enjoy as we are getting closer and closer to the end of our adventure.

Join our book's Discord space

Join the book's Discord Workspace for Latest updates, Offers, Tech happenings around the world, New Release and Sessions with the Authors:

https://discord.bpbonline.com

Chapter 13
Orleans

Introduction

Another chapter, another round in our way into this world.

In this chapter we will learn about Orleans, which is a cross-platform framework that can be used to build scalable and robust distributed interactive applications based on .Net.

So, to learn about it, we will see what it really is, learn a bit of Orleans history and how it can be used.

After that it is time to see what improvements and changes will .Net 7 bring to this framework, which can be very useful and interesting.

It is time to get ready and discover this framework and how it works. Get ready!

Meanwhile, we share you Orleans logo, in the following figure:

Figure 13.1: Orleans logo

Structure

The topics that will be covered in this chapter will be:

- What is Orleans
- How it can be used
- What it has new in .Net 7

Objectives

This chapter has the objective to learn about Orleans.

We will go through a definition of the framework, explaining what it is, and how it can be used.

Afterwards, we will see what It will bring new in .Net 7.

What is Orleans

When you think of Orleans you may think of the cities (in France Orléans and in USA, New Orleans), but it is more than it. It is a cross-platform framework that is used to build scalable and robust distributed interactive applications based on .Net.

It was created by the eXtreme Computing Group at Microsoft research and started by showing the Virtual Actor Model, which is a new approach on building distributed systems for the cloud.

The gaming franchise *Halo*, from which is shown a cover on *Figure 13.2*, was one of the first developments that used Orleans in its cloud services. Orleans core technology was transferred to the development company – 343 industries – becoming available as open source starting January 2015 – with the repository in GitHub.

Figure 13.2: Halo 4 game cover, one of the first with the use of Orleans in its cloud service

How and where to use Orleans

Orleans works based on **Grains**, which is, in terms of the Actor Model, the virtual actor. Meaning, the building block in any Orleans application is a Grain. The Grains can have identity, behaviour and state as seen in *Figure 13.3* taken from Microsoft Learn:

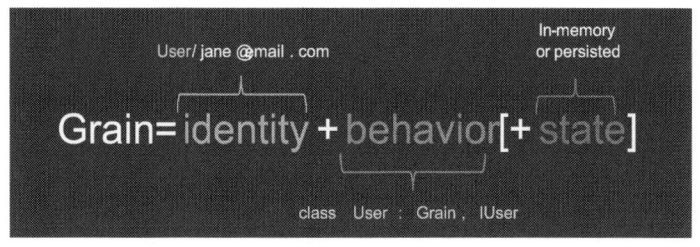

Figure 13.3: *Grains*

Identity is a used-defined key to make the grain always available to be invoked. A Grain can be invoked by other grains or external clients, and it is an instance of a class that will implement one or more of these interfaces:
- `IGrainWithGuidKey`
- `IGrainWithIntegerKey`
- `IGrainWithStringKey`
- `IGrainWithGuidCompoundKey`
- `IGrainWithIntegerCompoundKeys`

A Grain can have its state changed several times, but it will always be stored in memory while it is active, improving the performance.

Grain states can vary as seen in the following figure:

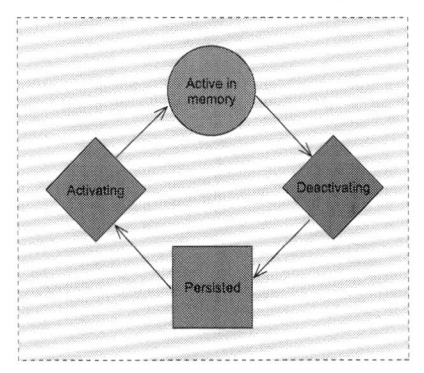

Figure 13.4: *Grains Lifecycle*

Other than Grains, Orleans works with **Silos**, that are hosts to one or more grains.

Normally, a group of silos will run as a cluster, to maintain scalability and fault tolerance. Doing this they will coordinate between each other so that the work can be distributed, and they will be able to detect and recover from failures.

Let us see an example of this cluster in *Figure 13.5*:

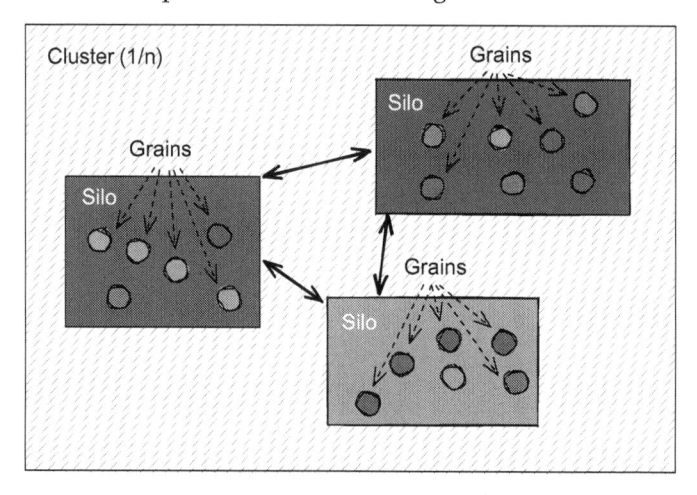

Figure 13.5: Cluster with Silos

So, after this first explanation, when can you use Orleans? It is recommended for use when building cloud-native apps that eventually need to be scaled. As seen before, one of Orleans implementation can be on Gaming, but also banking, chat applications, GPS tracking, shopping carts, and the like. It is used in Azure and besides the usage in Halo, it can be found also in Skype, Xbox, Gears of war and many other services.

Following is a figure with some of these applications/systems where it can be used:

Figure 13.6: Applications/Systems where Orleans is used

But what does Orleans include? It has some great features like:

- **Persistence**: When a state of a system outlives the process that created it. Orleans guarantees that the consistency is maintained, by keeping in memory, Grain states, to reduce storage access when read requests are made.
- **Distributed ACID (atomicity, consistency, isolation, durability) transactions**: Besides persistence, Grains can participate in this transactions, despite of the state they have stored.
- **Streams**: This help developers to process several data items in near-real-time. They don't need to be created or registered before a Grain or client publishes or subscribes to them. It is a very reliable process because it stores checkpoints that can later be reset to. Streams also have messages delivered to consumers in batches, thus improving efficiency and recovery performance.
- **Timers and Reminders**: Reminders are used to guarantee that some action can be completed at a future point even if the grain isn't activated at that time. Timers are the counterpart to reminders and can be used for high-frequency events, that don't require reliability.
- **Fault Tolerance**: Enables a system to operate, in the event of a failure occurs in some of its components.

Next, it is explained, with some examples from Microsoft Learn, how we can build an app with Orleans:

1. First you need to create a project using Visual Studio Code.
    i. You must start by creating minimal API project with .Net 7, using this command:
        1. `dotnet new web -o UrlShortener -f net7.0`
    ii. Then you need to open the project inside Visual Studio Code, with the following command:
        1. `cd UrlShortener`
        2. `code .`
    iii. Now, the project can be built and run from the terminal with **dotnet run** command.

2. Now, we must add Orleans to the project.

    i. Firstly, we must install the package, with this command:

    ```
    1.  dotnet add package Microsoft.Orleans.
        Server -v 7.0.0
    ```

    ii. Following, we need to add the using statements to the top of the **Program** class, as following:

    ```
    1.  using Microsoft.AspNetCore.Http.Extensions;
    2.  using Orleans.Runtime;
    ```

3. After this, we can now create Grains and Silos. First, we will create a grain to manage the shortened URL redirect.

    i. Inside **Program** class, we must add an interface definition so that it can be afterwards implemented:

    ```
    1.  public interface IUrlShortener-
        Grain : IGrainWithStringKey
    2.  {
    3.      Task SetUrl(string shortenedRoute-
        Segment, string fullUrl);
    4.      Task<string> GetUrl();
    5.  }
    ```

    ii. Following, it is time to create a class that will inherit from **Grain** class, which is provided by Orleans, and will implement the interface create in point 3.a).

    ```
    1.  public class UrlShortener-
        Grain : Grain, IUrlShortenerGrain
    2.  {
    3.      private KeyValue-
        Pair<string, string> _cache;
    4.
    5.      public Task SetUrl(string
        shortenedRouteSegment, string fullUrl)
    6.      {
    7.          _cache = new KeyValuePair
    ```

```
       <string, string>(shortenedRouteSegment,
       fullUrl);
8.            return Task.CompletedTask;
9.     }
10.
11.    public Task<string?> GetUrl()
12.    {
13.           return Task.FromResult(_cache.Value);
14.    }
15. }
```

    iii. We now have the Grain configured; it is time to set up the Silo. The first step is to add, at the top of Program class, the refactoring of the builder code to use Orleans, that will look like something like this:

```
1. var builder = WebApplication.CreateBuilder();
2.
3. builder.Host.UseOrleans(siloBuilder =>
4. {
5.    siloBuilder.UseLocalhostClustering();
6. });
7.
8. var app = builder.Build();
```

    iv. Next, it must be retrieved the instance of grain factory. Orleans has a default grain factory to manage the creation and retrieval of grains, by their identifiers. After the last line of code in point 3.c), we must add this in the following line:

```
1. var grainFactory = app.Services.GetRequiredService<IGrainFactory>();
```

4. Now, we must configure and create an API endpoint that will shorten URLs.

    i. In our code, after the existing "Hello World" endpoint, we must add this code:

```
1.  app.MapGet("/shorten/{*path}",
2.      async (IgrainFactory grains, HttpRe-
quest request, string path) =>
3.  {
4.      return Results.Ok();
5.  });
```

ii. Then, we must update the body of the GET method created in point 4.a). The code will use a GUID to create a random shortened route as a hexadecimal string, that will then be used as an identifier by the grain factory to create a new grain. Also, the shortened route segment and the original target URL will be stored in the grain instance. Then, a new URL with the shortened route segment will be assembled and returned to the user:

```
1.  app.MapGet("/shorten/{*path}",
2.      async (IgrainFactory grains, HttpRe-
quest request, string path) =>
3.  {
4.      var shortenedRouteSegment = Guid.
NewGuid().GetHashCode().ToString("X");
5.      var shortenerGrain = grains.Get-
Grain<IurlShortenerGrain>(shortenedRoute-
Segment);
6.      await shortenerGrain.
SetUrl(shortenedRouteSegment, path);
7.      var resultBuilder = new UriBuild-
er(request.GetEncodedUrl())
8.      {
9.          Path = $"/go/
{shortenedRouteSegment}"
10.     };
11.
12.     return Results.Ok(resultBuilder.
Uri);
13. });
```

iii. After this creation, it is needed to create another endpoint to redirect shortened URLs to the full address. This new endpoint will pass the shortened route segment as a URL path parameter:

```
1.  app.MapGet("/go/{shortenedRouteSegment}",
2.      async (IgrainFactory grains, string shortenedRouteSegment) =>
3.  {
4.      var shortenerGrain = grains.GetGrain<IurlShortenerGrain>(shortenedRouteSegment);
5.      var url = await shortenerGrain.GetUrl();
6.
7.      return Results.Redirect(url);
8.  });
```

iv. To test the app created, we can use the **dotnet run** command, that will display in the browser the "Hello World!" text.

v. In the address bar of the browser, we can test the shorten endpoint, which must reload and provide a shortened URL, that you can copy to the clipboard:

```
1.  {localhost}/shorten/https://microsoft.com
```

vi. Paste this shortened URL to the address bar and press enter, which should launch a reload and redirection to **https://microsoft.com**.

5. Working with Grains, it is needed to persist state, in order to ensure that data is safe between application restarts, grain deactivations and other situations. To persist data, Grains implement persistent state using this API:

```
1.  public interface IpersistentState<Tstate> where Tstate : new()
2.  {
```

```
3.     Tstate State { get; set; }
4.     string Etag { get; }
5.     Task ClearStateAsync();
6.     Task WriteStateAsync();
7.     Task ReadStateAsync();
8. }
```

i. These three methods that are used in the interface will help manage the **Tstate** object:

- **ClearStateAsync**: This clears the grain's state in storage.
- **WriteStateAsync**: This will persist the changes made to the state object. A change isn't automatically stored until this method is called.
- **ReadStateAsync**: This will be called automatically on grain activation, so it can surface state values to other components. It can still be called explicitly when needed to read the latest state in storage.

ii. The grain state can be used by declaring the objects we want to persist in the constructor of the grain. Also, they must have the **PersistentStateAttribute**, which will give them access to the API methods. This attribute will accept two parameters:

- **Name**: This is the name of the state object.
- **Storage Name**: This is the storage provider the object should be saved to.

Following is shown an example of this usage:

```
1. public class UrlShortener-
Grain : Grain, IurlShortenerGrain
2. {
3.     private readonly IpersistentState<K
eyValuePair<string, string>> _cache;
4.
5.     public UrlShortenerGrain(
```

```
6.      [PersistentState(
7.          stateName: "url",
8.          storageName: "urls")]
9.          IpersistentState<KeyValue-
Pair<string, string>> state)
10.     {
11.         _cache = state;
12.     }
13. }
```

iii. Beforehand persisting grain state objects in storage, it is needed to configure a silo storage provider. The basic configurations are handled by the **SiloBuilder** but following is shown as an example on this usage:

```
1. builder.Host.UseOrleans(siloBuilder =>
2. {
3.      siloBuilder.UseLocalhostClustering();
4.      siloBuilder.AddAzureBlobGrainStorage("urls",
5.          // Recommended: Connect to Blob Storage using DefaultAzureCredential
6.          options =>
7.          {
8.              options.ConfigureBlobServiceClient(new Uri("https://<your-account-name>.blob.core.windows.net"),
9.                  new DefaultAzureCredential());
10.         });
11.         // Connect to Blob Storage using Connection strings
12.         // options => options.ConfigureBlobServiceClient(connectionString));
13. });
```

6. Then, to configure how grains are stored by the app, we can modify the **UseOrleans** method, as shown in the following code sample:

```
1. builder.Host.UseOrleans(siloBuilder =>
2. {
3.     siloBuilder.UseLocalhostClustering();
4.     siloBuilder.AddMemoryGrainStorage("urls");
5. });
```

7. Also, we can update the grains so they can use persistent storage.

   i. In **UrlShortenerGrain** method, we must add a constructor and update the following as shown following:

```
1. private IPersistentState<KeyValue-
Pair<string, string>> _cache;
2.
3. public UrlShortenerGrain(
4.     [PersistentState(
5.         stateName: "url",
6.         storageName: "urls")]
7.         IPersistentState<KeyValue-
Pair<string, string>> state)
8. {
9.     _cache = state;
10. }
```

   ii. Then, we must update the grain method to use the new state field. The method **SetUrl** will assign the URL alias and the full URL to a **KeyValuePair** that will then be persisted in grain state. The **GetUrl** method will return the full URL from the **KeyValuePair** that is stored in the Grain, so it can be used by the application:

```
1. public async Task SetUrl(string
shortenedRouteSegment, string fullUrl)
```

```
2. {
3.     _cache.
State = new KeyValuePair<string, string>
(shortenedRouteSegment, fullUrl);
4.     await _cache.WriteStateAsync();
5. }
6.
7. public Task<string> GetUrl()
8. {
9.     return Task.FromResult(_cache.
State.Value);
10. }
```

What is new in Orleans in .Net 7

Orleans in this new 7.0 version will bring a programming model that will be simpler to use and will have POCO (plain old CLR object) Grains, being able to improve performance in up to 150%.

Also, it will be introduced new serialization and improvements in the immutability.

Orleans is being improved to allow support for the most popular storage mechanisms and databases and to have the ability to run anywhere ASP.Net Core can run. Microsoft wants Orleans to be top choice to enable .Net applications with cloud native, distributed capabilities without needing to learn a new framework.

But now let us see a bit more detailed what Orleans has new in .Net 7:

- **Improved development experience**: Orleans 7 will have some new packages that will simplify how you get started with new projects and solutions that depend on Orleans. In this version you no longer need to remember to reference **Microsoft.Orleans.CodeGenerator.MsBuild**, no matter if it is an abstraction or implementation project or a silo or client host project. NuGet package references are now extremely simplified:
    - Orleans client project will reference **Microsoft.Orleans.Client** package.

- o Orleans silo projects will reference **Microsoft.Orleans.Server** package.
- o **Microsoft.Orleans.Sdk** package will be referenced by Abstractions and any other Orleans-dependent project references.

- Simplified Grain and Stream identifications: In .Net 7, Grain identities will have the form type/key where both type and key are strings, which will simplify how it works and will improve support for generic grain types. Also, complexity was reduced because now we don't need a compound type for GrainIds so we can support keys that are Guid, long, string, Guid + string or long + string. The identity of a Grain now is simply a type and a key, both strings, instead of before, when a type was a numeric type code, a category and 3 bytes of generic type information. In previous versions, there were many ways to identify a Grain, as seen in this example from Microsoft Devblogs:

```
1.  public class PingGrain : Grain, IPingGrain
2.  {
3.      public ILogger<PingGrain> Logger { get; set; }
4.
5.      public PingGrain(ILogger<PingGrain> logger) => Logger = logger;
6.
7.      public Task ReceivePing(PingMessage message)
8.      {
9.          string grainId = this.GetGrainIdentity().PrimaryKeyString;
10.         Guid grainId = this.GetGrainIdentity().PrimaryKey;
11.         long grainId = this.GetGrainIdentity().PrimaryKeyLong;
12.
13.         // or...
```

```
14.
15.         string grainId = this.
    GetPrimaryKeyString();
16.         Guid grainId = this.GetPrimaryKey();
17.         long grainId = this.
    GetPrimaryKeyLong();
18.
19.         Logger.LogInformation($"{message.
    Message} from {grainId} at {message.
    Timestamp}.");
20.     }
21. }
```

Now, in .Net 7, it is much simpler. You just need to call **GetGrainId**, as following:

```
1. public class PingGrain : Grain, IPingGrain
2. {
3.     public ILogger<PingGrain> Logger { get; set; }
4.
5.     public PingGrain(ILogger<PingGrain> logger) => Logger = logger;
6.
7.     public Task ReceivePing(PingMessage message)
8.         => Task.Run(() => Logger.LogInformation($"{message.Message} from {this.GetGrainId()} at {message.Timestamp}."));
9. }
```

This is a good improvement and a great simplification that Microsoft brought to .Net 7. Regarding Streams, they are now too simply identified using string instead of Guid, which will allow more flexibility, especially when you work with declarative subscriptions.

These changes will make development simpler, since now **GrainId** and **StreamId** types are **public** and **GrainId** is able to identify any Grain.

Conclusion

In this chapter we have learned about Orleans.

We got to know what Orleans is, how it can be used and what it brings new in .Net 7.

You have learned a lot of new and interesting things we went through some examples and some interesting information that allows us to learn more about this framework, that can be very useful.

We hope this could have been interesting and that you have learned a lot, and also, that this knowledge will help you with .Net 7 and your job.

But, remain on your seat, as we are approaching our final target.

Following is time to learn about System.Devices, so get ready and relax before the following chapter on our journey.

Join our book's Discord space

Join the book's Discord Workspace for Latest updates, Offers, Tech happenings around the world, New Release and Sessions with the Authors:

https://discord.bpbonline.com

Chapter 14
Adding Specific Code Using System.Devices

Introduction

We are quite near the end of our journey.

After having learned a lot of new and interesting things regarding .Net 7 and its improvements and enhancements, we will go through System.Devices in this chapter.

System.Devices will help to enumerate all the devices and finding a specific device that can then be used in .Net.

We will go through some information on this topic, get to know what System.Devices is, learn on some specifics and how these can be used in .Net 7.

So, let us get ready to enter one of our last adventures.

Hope you enjoy it!

Structure

The topics that will be covered in this chapter will be:

- System.Devices

- How to use it with .Net 7

Objectives

This chapter has the objective to learn about **System.Devices** and some specific code related to it.

We will get to know what is **System.Devices** and we will see some specifics that can be used.

Also, we will see how we can add it in .Net 7.

System.Devices

You can use **System.Devices**, in .Net MAUI, using **IDeviceInfo** interface, that allows you to read information about the device where the application is running on.

This interface has got its default implementation available though the **DeviceInfo.Current** property. The interface and the class, are both contained in **Microsoft.Maui.Devices** namespace.

To read the Device information, you can use the following code example (which is taken from Microsoft learn):

```
1.  private void ReadDeviceInfo()
2.  {
3.      System.Text.StringBuilder sb = new System.Text.StringBuilder();
4.
5.      sb.AppendLine($"Model: {DeviceInfo.Current.Model}");
6.      sb.AppendLine($"Manufacturer: {DeviceInfo.Current.Manufacturer}");
7.      sb.AppendLine($"Name: {DeviceInfo.Name}");
8.      sb.AppendLine($"OS Version: {DeviceInfo.VersionString}");
9.      sb.AppendLine($"Refresh Rate: {DeviceInfo.Current}");
10.     sb.AppendLine($"Idiom: {DeviceInfo.Current.Idiom}");
```

Adding Specific Code Using System.Devices — 185

```
11.    sb.AppendLine($"Platform: {DeviceInfo.Current.
       Platform}");
12.
13.    bool isVirtual = DeviceInfo.Current.
       DeviceType switch
14.    {
15.        DeviceType.Physical => false,
16.        DeviceType.Virtual => true,
17.        _ => false
18.    };
19.
20.    sb.AppendLine($"Virtual device? {isVirtual}");
21.
22.    DisplayDeviceLabel.Text = sb.ToString();
23. }
```

You can check what Operating System the application is running by using the **DevicePlatform** type, that contains a property for each one:

- **DevicePlatform.Android**
- **DevicePlatform.iOS**
- **DevicePlatform.macOS**
- **DevicePlatform.MacCatalyst**
- **DevicePlatform.tvOS**
- **DevicePlatform.Tizen**
- **DevicePlatform.WinUI**
- **DevicePlatform.watchOS**
- **DevicePlatform.Unknown**

You can also get the type of device on which your platform is running on. To get it, you can use DeviceIdiom type, which provides a property for each type of device:

- **DeviceIdiom.Phone**
- **DeviceIdiom.Tablet**
- **DeviceIdiom.Desktop**

- **DeviceIdiom.TV**
- **DeviceIdiom.Watch**
- **DeviceIdiom.Unknown**

There is also the possibility to identify if your device is physical or virtual, as seen in this following Microsoft Learn example:

```
1. bool isVirtual = DeviceInfo.Current.DeviceType switch
2. {
3.     DeviceType.Physical => false,
4.     DeviceType.Virtual => true,
5.     _ => false
6. };
```

Also, in .Net MAUI, you can access Display Information on the device the application is running. By using **IDeviceDisplay. MainDisplayInfo** property, you will receive information about the screen and orientation.

Check how it can be done in this example, which was once again, taken from Microsoft Learn:

```
1. private void ReadDeviceDisplay()
2. {
3.     System.Text.StringBuilder sb = new System.Text.StringBuilder();
4.
5.     sb.AppendLine($"Pixel width: {DeviceDisplay.Current.MainDisplayInfo.Width} / Pixel Height: {DeviceDisplay.Current.MainDisplayInfo.Height}");
6.     sb.AppendLine($"Density: {DeviceDisplay.Current.MainDisplayInfo.Density}");
7.     sb.AppendLine($"Orientation: {DeviceDisplay.Current.MainDisplayInfo.Orientation}");
8.     sb.AppendLine($"Rotation: {DeviceDisplay.Current.MainDisplayInfo.Rotation}");
9.     sb.AppendLine($"Refresh Rate: {DeviceDisplay.Current.MainDisplayInfo.RefreshRate}");
```

Adding Specific Code Using System.Devices ▪ 187

```
10.
11.     DisplayDetailsLabel.Text = sb.ToString();
12. }
```

There is still the possibility to, in your application, avoid the device's screen to lock, which can be useful. You will just need to set the property **IDeviceDisplay.KeepScreenOn** to true.

Next is an example on how to do it:

```
1. private void AlwaysOnSwitch_
   Toggled(object sender, ToggledEventArgs e) =>
2.     DeviceDisplay.Current.
   KeepScreenOn = AlwaysOnSwitch.IsToggled;
```

Another point on which **System.Devices** can be interesting, and using .Net MAUI, is to get sensors information.

This can be useful, for example if you are developing a game, because you will be able to get information on **SensorSpeed**. It has got the following enumerations:

- **Fastest**: This will return the sensor data as fast as possible
- **Game**: This will return the rate, most suitable for games
- **Default**: This will return the default rate, that can be useful when you need to change screen orientation
- **UI**: This will return rate that can be more suitable for general user interface

You will be able to access Device Information about some useful sensor:

- **Accelerometer**: This will measure the acceleration of the device in its three axes. It will return information on how the user is moving the device.

    Microsoft.Maui.Devices.Sensors namespace contains **IAccelerometer** interface and also **Accelerometer** class.

    The interface is available through **Accelerometer.Default** property.

    Following is an example, from Microsoft Learn, on how to use this Sensor:

```csharp
1. public void ToggleAccelerometer()
2. {
3.     if (Accelerometer.Default.IsSupported)
4.     {
5.         if (!Accelerometer.Default.IsMonitoring)
6.         {
7.             // Turn on accelerometer
8.             Accelerometer.Default.ReadingChanged += Accelerometer_ReadingChanged;
9.             Accelerometer.Default.Start(SensorSpeed.UI);
10.        }
11.        else
12.        {
13.            // Turn off accelerometer
14.            Accelerometer.Default.Stop();
15.            Accelerometer.Default.ReadingChanged -= Accelerometer_ReadingChanged;
16.        }
17.    }
18. }
19.
20. private void Accelerometer_ReadingChanged(object sender, AccelerometerChangedEventArgs e)
21. {
22.     // Update UI Label with accelerometer state
23.     AccelLabel.TextColor = Colors.Green;
24.     AccelLabel.Text = $"Accel: {e.Reading}";
25. }
```

- **Barometer**: This will measure the ambient air pressure. It will return information on the current air pressure, starting by the first time the user starts monitoring it and then, every time the pressure changes.

    Microsoft.Maui.Devices.Sensors namespace contains **IBarometer** interface and also **Barometer** class.

    The interface is available through **Barometer.Default** property.

    Next is shown an example, from Microsoft Learn, on how to use this Sensor:

```
1.  public void ToggleBarometer()
2.  {
3.      if (Barometer.Default.IsSupported)
4.      {
5.          if (!Barometer.Default.IsMonitoring)
6.          {
7.              // Turn on accelerometer
8.              Barometer.Default.ReadingChanged += Barometer_ReadingChanged;
9.              Barometer.Default.Start(SensorSpeed.UI);
10.         }
11.         else
12.         {
13.             // Turn off accelerometer
14.             Barometer.Default.Stop();
15.             Barometer.Default.ReadingChanged -= Barometer_ReadingChanged;
16.         }
17.     }
18. }
19.
20. private void Barometer_ReadingChanged(object sender, BarometerChangedEventArgs e)
```

```
21. {
22.     // Update UI Label with barometer state
23.     BarometerLabel.TextColor = Colors.Green;
24.     BarometerLabel.Text = $"Barometer: {e.Reading}";
25. }
```

- **Compass**: This will measure the device's magnetic north heading.

    Microsoft.Maui.Devices.Sensors namespace contains **ICompass** interface and also **Compass** class.

    The interface is available through **Compass.Default** property.

    It is shown an example, from Microsoft Learn, on how to use this Sensor:

```
1.  private void ToggleCompass()
2.  {
3.      if (Compass.Default.IsSupported)
4.      {
5.          if (!Compass.Default.IsMonitoring)
6.          {
7.              // Turn on compass
8.              Compass.Default.ReadingChanged += Compass_ReadingChanged;
9.              Compass.Default.Start(SensorSpeed.UI);
10.         }
11.         else
12.         {
13.             // Turn off compass
14.             Compass.Default.Stop();
15.             Compass.Default.ReadingChanged -= Compass_ReadingChanged;
16.         }
```

Adding Specific Code Using System.Devices ▪ 191

```
17.    }
18. }
19.
20. private void Compass_ReadingChanged(ob-
    ject sender, CompassChangedEventArgs e)
21. {
22.     // Update UI Label with compass state
23.     CompassLabel.TextColor = Colors.Green;
24.     CompassLabel.Text = $"Compass: {e.
    Reading}";
25. }
```

- **Shake**: This will measure when the device is shaken and will use, not Shake sensor, but the accelerometer.

    Microsoft.Maui.Devices.Sensors namespace contains **IAccelerometer** interface and also **Accelerometer** class.

    The interface is available through **Accelerometer.Default** property.

    Next is shown an example, from Microsoft Learn, on how to use this Sensor:

```
1. private void ToggleShake()
2. {
3.     if (Accelerometer.Default.IsSupported)
4.     {
5.         if (!Accelerometer.Default.
    IsMonitoring)
6.         {
7.             // Turn on compass
8.             Accelerometer.Default.
    ShakeDetected += Accelerometer_ShakeDetected;
9.             Accelerometer.Default.
    Start(SensorSpeed.Game);
10.        }
11.        else
12.        {
```

```
13.             // Turn off compass
14.             Accelerometer.Default.Stop();
15.             Accelerometer.Default.
    ShakeDetected -= Accelerometer_ShakeDetected;
16.         }
17.     }
18. }
19.
20. private void Accelerometer_
    ShakeDetected(object sender, EventArgs e)
21. {
22.     // Update UI Label with a "shaked detect-
    ed" notice, in a randomized color
23.     ShakeLabel.TextColor = new Color(Random.
    Shared.Next(256), Random.Shared.
    Next(256), Random.Shared.Next(256));
24.     ShakeLabel.Text = $"Shake detected";
25. }
```

- **Gyroscope**: This will measure the angular rotation speed around the device's three primary axes.

  Microsoft.Maui.Devices.Sensors namespace contains **IGyroscope** interface and also **Gyroscope** class.

  The interface is available through **Gyroscope.Default** property.

  Next is shown an example, from Microsoft Learn, on how to use this Sensor:

```
1. private void ToggleGyroscope()
2. {
3.     if (Gyroscope.Default.IsSupported)
4.     {
5.         if (!Gyroscope.Default.IsMonitoring)
6.         {
7.             // Turn on compass
8.             Gyroscope.Default.
```

Adding Specific Code Using System.Devices ■ 193

```
        ReadingChanged += Gyroscope_ReadingChanged;
9.          Gyroscope.Default.
   Start(SensorSpeed.UI);
10.         }
11.         else
12.         {
13.             // Turn off compass
14.             Gyroscope.Default.Stop();
15.             Gyroscope.Default.
   ReadingChanged -= Gyroscope_ReadingChanged;
16.         }
17.     }
18. }
19.
20. private void Gyroscope_ReadingChanged(object sender, GyroscopeChangedEventArgs e)
21. {
22.     // Update UI Label with gyroscope state
23.     GyroscopeLabel.TextColor = Colors.Green;
24.     GyroscopeLabel.Text = $"Gyroscope: {e.Reading}";
25. }
```

- **Magnetometer**: This will indicate the device's orientation relative to Earth's magnetic field.

  Microsoft.Maui.Devices.Sensors namespace contains **IMagnetometer** interface and also **Magnetometer** class.

  The interface is available through **Magnetometer.Default** property.

  Next is shown an example, from Microsoft Learn, on how to use this Sensor:

```
1. private void ToggleMagnetometer()
2. {
3.     if (Magnetometer.Default.IsSupported)
```

```
4.     {
5.         if (!Magnetometer.Default.IsMonitoring)
6.         {
7.             // Turn on compass
8.             Magnetometer.Default.
   ReadingChanged += Magnetometer_ReadingChanged;
9.             Magnetometer.Default.
   Start(SensorSpeed.UI);
10.        }
11.        else
12.        {
13.            // Turn off compass
14.            Magnetometer.Default.Stop();
15.            Magnetometer.Default.
   ReadingChanged -= Magnetometer_ReadingChanged;
16.        }
17.    }
18. }
19.
20. private void Magnetometer_ReadingChanged(object sender, MagnetometerChangedEventArgs e)
21. {
22.     // Update UI Label with magnetometer state
23.     MagnetometerLabel.TextColor = Colors.Green;
24.     MagnetometerLabel.
   Text = $"Magnetometer: {e.Reading}";
25. }
```

- **Orientation**: This will monitor the device's orientation in 3D space.

  Microsoft.Maui.Devices.Sensors namespace contains **IOrientationSensor** interface and also **OrientationSensor** class.

  The interface is available through **OrientationSensor. Default** property.

Adding Specific Code Using System.Devices ■ 195

Next is shown an example, from Microsoft Learn, on how to use this Sensor:

```
1. private void ToggleOrientation()
2. {
3.     if (OrientationSensor.Default.IsSupported)
4.     {
5.         if (!OrientationSensor.Default.IsMonitoring)
6.         {
7.             // Turn on compass
8.             OrientationSensor.Default.ReadingChanged += Orientation_ReadingChanged;
9.             OrientationSensor.Default.Start(SensorSpeed.UI);
10.        }
11.        else
12.        {
13.            // Turn off compass
14.            OrientationSensor.Default.Stop();
15.            OrientationSensor.Default.ReadingChanged -= Orientation_ReadingChanged;
16.        }
17.    }
18. }
19.
20. private void Orientation_ReadingChanged(object sender, OrientationSensorChangedEventArgs e)
21. {
22.     // Update UI Label with orientation state
23.     OrientationLabel.TextColor = Colors.Green;
24.     OrientationLabel.Text = $"Orientation: {e.Reading}";
25. }
```

Conclusion

In this chapter we have learned about System.Devices.

The next chapter will be our final one, and it will contain some questions and possible answers that will help you in interviews, to get a job in .Net 7.

But before getting to that, let us wrap up about what we have learned here: we have seen a bit of what System.Devices is, and some examples or properties that can be used and accessed in .Net 7, using for example, .Net MAUI.

Hoe you have enjoyed it and learned with it.

Be ready now for the questions and answers that hopefully will help you go through with your desire to get a job in programming and using .Net 7.

Join our book's Discord space

Join the book's Discord Workspace for Latest updates, Offers, Tech happenings around the world, New Release and Sessions with the Authors:

https://discord.bpbonline.com

CHAPTER 15
Possible Questions and Answers

Introduction

Finally we are here with the last chapter of this book.

With this journey, now it is time to go through some questions and answers about .Net 7 and about what we have learned throughout this book.

Remember the history on .Net, the new features that .Net 7 brings, how to write our first program and design the views, controllers, and Models, using MVC – but never forget Razor. Don't forget the things we have learned on .Net MAUI, Blazor or desktop applications and how to communicate with the views.

There's also the learning path we have made on SignalR, databases, Orleans and lastly System.Devices.

Now, with all this in mind, we will show some questions that, hopefully can help you on job seeking, when asked by a recruiter.

Let us get going and see what questions we can have.

Figure 15.1: *Q & A on an interview*

Structure

The topics that will be covered in this chapter will be:

- Possible questions and answers on .Net 7

Objectives

This chapter has the objective to provide you with some questions and possible answers on .Net 7, when you're have an interview or wants to seek a job.

Possible questions and answers

While on job seeking, we can come across some issues and some questions made by recruiters and job hunters.

So, in this chapter, we will try to help by showing some possible questions and answers that can help you getting a job on .Net 7.

Besides questions directly related to .Net 7, of course, there are some more generic on .Net that will always be of help.

1. **What is .Net Framework?**

    A: .Net framework is an abstraction that contains generic functionalities executed on a CLR – Common Language Runtime, to provide user interface, data access, database connectivity, cryptography, web application development, numeric algorithms, and network communications. All of this, can be combined in the source code that is created by programmers and software engineers, allowing them to create cloud apps, console apps, web apps, APIs, desktop apps, games, mobile apps, windows apps, machine learning and IoT applications. .Net 7 is not a framework but a Core .Net version that uses its framework and brings several improvements to the later ones.

2. **What are some of the improvements that .Net 7 brings?**

    A: .Net 7 will bring some improvements to its later versions. Some of them will focus on Blazor, with the addition of a new loading page, modification of data bindings, improvements on virtualization, a navigation manager to pass states, additional cryptography support with more cryptographic algorithms, a new problem details service and updates on diagnostics middleware. Other changes and improvements in .Net 7 are made on Minimal APIs, with the introduction of IResult interface that will represent minimal APIs return values that will not be implicitly supported, to serialize the returned object to HTTP response, with the use of JSON. Also, for minimal APIs, there are some OpenAPI improvements that will now include support to allow APIs to interact with the OpenAPI specification in minimal APIs. It will also be introduced self-describing minimal APIs to allow its types to be used not only in route handlers, but also in endpoint metadata. Finally, regarding minimal APIs, it will be introduced the possibility to return multiple result types.

    Another improvement will be made on MVC and Razor Pages that will now have minimal APIs added to the model binding, making it possible to inject services into the action method, instead of having to inject it exclusively on the controller's constructor.

    Other thing that Microsoft improved is link generation, turning it more type-safe, allowing to pass generic variant.

    Finally, there will be some new libraries added, new nullable annotations for Microsoft.Extensions, improvements and new APIs for System.Text.RegularExpressions, a new LibraryImport Generator, and some improvements also on .Net MAUI, JSON, JWT authentication configurations and the introduction of C# 11.

3. **What is MVC?**

   A: MVC is an architecture used to build .Net applications, that works with three main components, that interact with each other, giving the architecture its name: Model, View, Controller.

   Model is the MVC part that, normally, will contain data and the related logic. It will contain database interaction and will receive information from the controller, retrieving it, so that it can be shown in the view.

   View is the UI part of the application. It will gather data from the models to display on the screen for allowing users to interact.

   Finally, the Controller, is the part where user interactions will be handled, and where the responses for the user input are worked on, to be rendered and displayed back to the view. It will be the "bridge" between Model and View.

4. **What is .Net MAUI?**

   A: .Net MAUI is a new Multi-Platform Application User Interface, which means, it is a framework that allow working cross-platforms and creating native mobile and desktop applications using C# and XAML.

   It will replace the use of Xamarin and will be useful to help creating an application that, with a single shared code base can be used cross-platform apps, like iOS, macOS, Android or Windows or if you want to share a UI layout and design or code, tests, and business logic between these different platforms.

   This can be achieved with the single framework that .Net MAUI provides, for building UIs for mobile and desktop apps. With it you only need to write the code once, and it will run in any of the platforms.

5. **What are the new functionalities of .Net MAUI?**

   A: In .Net 7, .Net MAUI will include a Map control that can be added to the project and will allow displaying maps and making annotations, using the native map for each mobile platform. There are also some desktop improvements, to enhance the user experience when using these applications. You can now, for example, add context menus, tooltips, pointer gestures, right-click mapping on tap gestures and have more control over the window size.

6. **What is Blazor?**

    A: Blazor is a feature of ASP.Net that extends its framework, with tools and libraries for building web apps, and interactive web User Interfaces, using C#, instead of JavaScript. These apps will be composed of reusable web UI components, implemented in C#, HTML and CSS, and will allow to write C# code both on client and server side, making it easy to share the code and the libraries.

    Blazor can be executed directly in the browser, running there the client-side, using WebAssembly, making it possible to re-use and share code and libraries from server-side parts of your application.

    This Blazor WebAssembly, also called WASM, is a single-page app framework that is used to build interactive client-side web apps using .Net and is optimized to allow fast download and maximum execution spend, being supported in browsers without the need for plugins.

7. **Can you talk about the new features that Blazor brings in .Net 7?**

    A: Blazor brings some improvements in .Net 7, mainly regarding the Web Assembly with a new UI construct, two new CSS custom properties to show the percentage of app files loaded and the same value but rounded to the nearest whole number. Also, at Data Binding, with new modifiers: @bind:after, @bind:get and @bind:set, which will allow to execute async code after the binding and to simplify the binding between component parameters and underlying UI elements.

    Another improvement that is made in Blazor is on Virtualize that will use a spacer element to define vertical height of the scroll region enclosed in div element by default. Also, .Net 7 has improvements in Blazor, on Navigation, by using a NavigationManager to enable simple communication between different pages and a LocationChanging event to implement logic that occurs begore navigation takes place.

Finally, there are some improvements made on Blazor Templates, simplifying their structure, and redesigning themes, and implementing an Empty Template, simpler than the existing ones, with less pre-existing code and UI.

8. **What is Blazor Hybrid?**

    A: Blazor Hybrid is an interconnection with .Net MAUI, that will help building interactive client-side web User Interface with .Net in an ASP .Net core application, allowing to blend desktop and mobile native client frameworks with .Net.

    In .Net MAUI it will exist a BlazorWebView control that will render Razor Components into an embedded Web View, allowing the reutilisation of one set of Web UI components across different platforms.

9. **In creating desktop UIs, what is WinUI 3?**

    A: Win UI is Windows User Interface, and it is a framework library used for Windows Desktop apps. The version 3 is the latest one and it is recommended to use with .Net 7. It is available as part of Windows App SDK, which gives a set of APIs and tools to be used by any C++ Win32 or C# .Net application, in several Windows Operating System versions.

10. **What is MVVM?**

    A: MVVM is an architectural pattern to simplify the separation of the graphic interface and the business logic and stands for Model-View-ViewModel. In this pattern, we have a Model, that represents a domain model or data access layer, a View that represents structure, layout, and appearance of what is seen by the user. It will show the representation of the model and will receive a user interaction, passing the handling of these interactions to the ViewModel, using data binding. The Binder that ViewModel uses to automate the communication between View and the properties in the ViewModel, is a markup language called **eXtensible Application Markup Language (XAML)**.

11. **What is SignalR?**

    A: SignalR is an ASP.Net library that helps developers to add real-time functionalities into web applications. It will allow web functionalities to send content to all end-users, instead of just getting the server to wait for the client requests.

It can be used for example, in a chat application, to send messages or notifications, to several users at the same time.

SignalR has got some benefits like bi-directional communication between one server and many clients at a time, allowing the broadcast of messages to one or several clients, efficiency, and simplicity to send notifications, feed updates, alert messages or product offers and providing great user experience.

12. **What are the most used databases in .Net Projects?**

    A: In .Net projects we can interact with several databases but, the most used are SQL Server, MySQL, and PostgreSQL.

    SQL Server, because it is Microsoft proprietary, and it is the first one that Entity Framework is developed for, and is the most common to use and the more recommended. You can also use SQL Server Developer Edition for free, which is a plus.

    MySQL remains open source, despite being acquired by Oracle in 2010, is the second most used.

    Finally, PostgreSQL, who is been gaining lots of fans, due to being open source and with a permissive license, is quite popular and is the third most used.

13. **How can you use and define database connections?**

    A: Database connections can be set on **appsettings.json** or defined in Azure, if you're using it. This is always more secure and can turn database access faster and simplifying the usage.

    You can also define scopes, authentication, and authorizations on **Startup.cs** or **Program.cs**.

14. **What is Orleans?**

    A: Orleans is a cross-platform framework that is used to build scalable and robust distributed interactive applications based on .Net. It has a Virtual Actor Model, which is a new approach on building distributed systems for the cloud.

    It is used in several games, including Halo franchise, which was one of the first developments to use Orleans.

Orleans works based on Grains, which can represent, in the Model used by the framework, the Virtual Actor. These Grains can have identity, behaviour, and state.

Identity is a user-defined key to make the grain always available when invoked.

Orleans also works with Silos, which are hosts to one or more grains and normally, a group of silos will run as cluster, to maintain scalability and fault tolerance. With this, they will coordinate between each other so that the work can be distributed, and they'll be able to detect and recover from failures.

Conclusion

In this chapter we have seen some possible questions and answers that will hopefully help you getting a job in .Net 7.

We hope this has been a good journey and that this book will be a great help for you, for the readers, who are fond of learning more on .Net 7, and in some general points of .Net. With this, we expect to help on finding a new job and be one of the great .Net programmers.

This book was such an interesting quest for me, and I have also learned a lot about .Net and about .Net 7 and its improvements. I am sure Microsoft will keep on helping us and giving us more tools to improve our developments and enhance the applications we, as developers, create for our users, allowing them to have more free time and applications more and more user friendly and user oriented.

I truly hope you will enjoy reading it as much as I have enjoyed writing it and learning from it.

Good Luck to your .Net 7 Job Seeking!

Join our book's Discord space

Join the book's Discord Workspace for Latest updates, Offers, Tech happenings around the world, New Release and Sessions with the Authors:

https://discord.bpbonline.com

Index

Symbols
.Net 6
  versus .Net 7 20
.Net 6 example
  about 4
  add services 6, 7
  middleware integration 4, 5
  routing 5, 6
.Net 7
  about 198
  Blazor, using 100-102
  improvements 199
  versus .Net 6 20
.Net 7 application
  .Net MAUI, using 91-95
.Net 7 features
  about 10
  additional cryptography 13
  Blazor 10
  data binding modifiers 11, 12

diagnostics middleware
  update 13
links 17
minimal API 13, 14
Model View Controller
  (MVC) 17
multiple result types,
  returning 16
navigation manager 12
OpenAPI improvement 15
page loading 11
problem details service 13
self-describing minimal
  APIs 15, 16
typed results 14
virtualization
  improvement 12
.Net 7 improvement
  to SignalR 152-154

.Net 7 project
  creating 28-32
  implementing 41-43
.Net 7 solution
  creating 28-32
.Net Framework 198, 199
.Net history 2, 3
.Net MAUI
  about 20, 21, 85, 200
  functionalities 200
  native packages 86
  set of controls 87
  using, in .Net 7 application 91-95
  WinUI, using 115, 116
  working 86
.Net MAUI functionalities
  about 87
  desktop improvement 88-91
  maps 87, 88
.Net MAUI platform-specific functionalities, for Android
  for application class 98
  for pages 97
  for views 97
.Net MAUI platform-specific functionalities, for iOS
  for application class 97
  for layouts 97
  for pages 96
  for views 96
.Net MAUI platform-specific functionalities, for Windows
  for application class 97
  for layouts 97
  for pages 97
  for views 97

.Net projects databases
  about 203
  MySQL 203
  PostgreSQL 203
  SQL Server 203

A

accelerometer 187
Ahead-Of-Time (AOT) 126
application program
  tests and debug, performing 80, 81
Application Programming Interface (APIs) 10
ASP.Net
  using, in SignalR 147-151
ASP.Net Core application
  SignalR, working 143, 144

B

barometer 189
Blazor 201
  about 10, 20, 21, 100
  features, in .Net 7 201
  in .Net 7 100, 102
Blazor for .Net 7
  about 103
  data binding 104
  navigation 104
  templates 104
  virtualize 104
  WebAssembly 103
Blazor Hybrid 105, 106, 202
Blazor WebAssembly (WASM) 101, 201

C

C# 11
  about 24
  features 24, 25
cloud native and containers 21

Index

code and libraries
  sharing 106
compass 190
Controller
  creating 64-67
  integrating, with View 67-72
Create, Read, Update, Delete (CRUD) 156
custom database template 166

D

database
  adding 156-160
  using 160, 161
database connections
  defining 203
  using 203
database types
  MySQL 157
  PostgreSQL 157
  SQL Server 157
Desktop UI
  about 114, 115
  Win32 116
  Windows Forms 117
  WinUI 3 115
Document Object Model (DOM) 101

E

Entity framework 7 161-163
Entity Framework (EF)
  about 161
  events 164
  interceptors 163
ExecuteDelete method 162
ExecuteUpdate method 162
eXtensible Application Markup Language (XAML) 139, 202

G

Grain 169
gyroscope 192

H

HubConnection class 144, 146

I

Internet Information System (IIS) 43

J

JavaScript Interop 106, 107, 110
JavaScript module functions
  afterStarted 110
  beforeStart(options, extensions) 110
JSON 22
JSON columns 164, 165
JWT authentication configuration 23

L

libraries
  LibraryImportGenerator 19, 20
  nullable annotations for Microsoft. Extensions 18
  System.Text.RegularExpressions improvement 19
LibraryImportGenerator 19, 20
long pooling 146

M

magnetometer 193
Model class
  adding 72-76
  creating 72
  using 72
Model View Controller (MVC)
  about 17, 46-49, 137, 200
  Controller to View method 138

Model to View method 137
View to View method 138
Model-View-
    ViewModel (MVVM)
    125, 138, 139, 161, 202
Multi-platform Application
    User Interface (MAUI) 83
MySQL 157, 203

N
Nullable annotations for
    Microsoft. Extensions 18

O
orientation 194, 195
Orleans
    about 168, 203, 204
    in .Net 7 179-181
    used, for building app 171-178
    using 169, 170
Orleans features
    distributed ACID
        transactions 171
    fault tolerance 171
    persistence 171
    streams 171
    timers and reminders 171

P
pages
    adding 33, 37-41
    configuring 33
    interacting between 37-41
    minimal APIs, using 36, 37
    Solution Explorer,
        navigating through 35
    view Index.cshtml,
        modifying 34, 35
partial view
    creating 52
PostgreSQL 157, 203

R
Razor pages 50-52

S
SetProperty method 163
shake sensor 191
SignalR
    about 142, 202, 203
    advantages 146, 147
    ASP.Net, using 147-151
    benefits 143
    features 146
    .Net 7 improvement 152-154
    usage 142, 143
    working, in ASP.Net Core
        application 143, 144
SQL Server 157, 203
System.Devices 184-187
System.Text.RegularExpressions
    improvement 19

T
Tstate object methods
    ClearStateAsync 176
    ReadStateAsync 176
    WriteStateAsync 176

U
unit tests
    about 78-80
    advantages 81, 82
User Interface (UI) 11, 86

V
View
    benefits 129
    communicating with 128, 129
    controller, interacting
        with 129-131
    creating 46
    creating, in Razor pages 50-61
    creating, with MVC 46-58

Index 209

data, passing 131-136
partial view, creating 52
used, for integrating
    Controller 67-72
ViewBag approach 135
ViewData approach 134
Visual Studio
    Magazine (VSM) 21

W

WebSockets 146
Win32 116
Windows Forms 117
Windows forms improvements,
    in .Net 7 123-126
Windows
    Presentation Foundation
    (WPF) 105, 125
Windows UI (WinUI)
  about 113
  using, on .Net MAUI 115, 116
WinUI 3
  about 115, 202
  project, creating 117-123

Made in the USA
Columbia, SC
25 May 2023